MAKING MILLIONS ON THE STREETS OF JAPAN

Luke Barisu

MINERVA PRESS
LONDON
ATLANTA MONTREUX SYDNEY

MAKING MILLIONS ON THE STREETS OF JAPAN
Copyright © Luke Barisu 1998

All Rights Reserved

No part of this book may be reproduced in any form
by photocopying or by any electronic or mechanical means,
including information storage or retrieval systems,
without permission in writing from both the copyright owner
and the publisher of this book.

ISBN 1 75410 406 0

First Published 1998 by
MINERVA PRESS
195 Knightsbridge
London SW7 1RE

Printed in Great Britain for Minerva Press

MAKING MILLIONS ON
THE STREETS OF JAPAN

Street-Sellers' Dictionary

arigatou gozaimashita	thank you (*doumo* very)
basho-dai	pitch payment
★basta	shop/stall (Hebrew expression)
ben	dialect
bentou	lunch-box
bounenkai	year end party
chijin naka ni mo reigi ari	there are formalities even among friends
daijoobu desu, mo tomodachi ni natte kita	it's all right, we're friends now
dame	forbidden/prohibited/bad
dojo	martial arts hall
doko (kara kimashita ka)?	where (are you from)?
dou desu ka	how about it?
en-yen (Y) sen en	one thousand yen
furin	love affair
★gai-jin	foreigner/alien
genki	healthy/fit/well
geta	Japanese clogs
gochisosama deshita	thank you for the meal (lit. it was a feast)
hansei	deep remorse
★hashigo	ladder (idiom. pub crawl)
hon-mono	genuine article
hi-gawari-teishoku	dish of the day
hima	not busy/free

ikura (desu ka)?	how much (does it cost)?
irashaimase!	may I help you? (lit. welcome!)
ishi no ne ni mo san nen	(lit. you have to sit on a stone for three years)
isogashii	busy
ittadakimasu	bon appetit
*izakaya	Japanese pub
Kagoshima no keisatsu wa hima dakara	because the kagoshima police have time on their hands
kawari-mono	different/strange person
keisatsu	police
kenba	room inspection
kimi	you (towards inferiors)
kimi wa jubbun asondekita	you've had your fill of fun
kimi ni aisatsu suru hitsuyou ga nai	I don't have to introduce myself to you
*kissaten	coffee shop
kokusai-teki	international
konnichiwa	hello
konbanwa	good evening
koukai	regret
kushi-yaki	grilled meat on a skewer
makeru	to give a discount
maa maa	so-so
mada daijoobu ka?	are you still all right?
mama san	snaku manageress
manga	comic book
mata (ne!)	again (see you again)
matsu (chotto matte kudasai)	to wait (please wait a moment)
*mizu-shoubai	night entertainment business (lit. water business)

nan ya?	what?
nise-mono	fake/imitation
o hanami	flower viewing
o-jiisan	old man
o-mae	you (towards inferiors)
omou	to think
onsen	hot spring bath
o-shirabe	investigative interview
o-taku	you (honorific/formal)
pachinko	Japanese slot machine (gambling game)
raamen	Chinese noodles
Renga-Doori	Brick Street
rotenshou	street-shop business
*saka-riba	nightlife area
sakura	cherry blossom
*san	Mr/Mrs/Ms
sayonara	goodbye
senpai	senior
*sentou	bath-house
sensei	teacher
shachou	company president
Shimotori	Kumamoto's main street
shinnenkai	New Year party
shitsurei shimashita	goodbye (lit. sorry I was rude)
shalom	hello (Hebrew)
shoubai (wa dou desu ka?)	business (how's business?)
skebe	lascivious person
*snaku	hostess karaoke bar
sumimasen	excuse me/I'm sorry
taishita koto nai	not important, nothing special
taiso no jikan	exercise period
takai	expensive

tako-yaki	grilled octopus
tatami	straw mats
Tenmonkan	Kagoshima's main street
uranai	fortune-telling/palm reading
wakarimashita	I see/understand
yaki-niku	grilled beef
yakitori	grilled chicken (on a skewer)
★yakuza	Japanese mafia
yasui	cheap
yatai	open-air night pub
yukata	Japanese kimono-type robe

★ denotes the most frequently used expressions in this book.

Prologue

Street-selling, a world-wide phenomenon, must surely rank among the least glamorous of professions. Having to stand for long hours in all winds and weathers, snubbed by the majority, and metaphorically scraped off the shoe of a minority, certainly does appear rather uninviting. However, freedom from official constraints, as well as endless opportunities for spontaneous sociability, are just two of the points often cited in its favour, while the third, and undoubtedly the most important factor, frequently remains unspoken; it is a real money-spinner, if not for the seller, then for the boss behind him.

Whereas the registered traders at organised local weekly markets up and down Britain are accorded a certain collective respectability, their pavement counterparts tend to be regarded with disdain. The former are seen as a vital and integral part of culture, while the latter are viewed by many as little more than parasites. This has something to do, no doubt, with legitimacy; the first pays for his pitch but the second frequently does not.

Whether it be a bedraggled rose seller on the A40, a lonely cockney souvenir merchant opposite Bond Street Tube Station or a homeless vendor of *The Big Issue* in the heart of Glasgow, the public tendency to pity them is enormous. Little do most people realise that the owner behind number one annually yields tens of thousands of pounds, number two holidays three months of the year in his luxury villa in America and, if the media is to be believed, the likes of number three and their boss are better off than all of us put together.

If prolonged international travel is your priority in life, then temporarily selling anything from melons in Biarritz to silk ties in Kowloon can prove an effective means to an end. However, in recent years, for those wishing to combine a lengthy cultural experience with some really serious street money, the islands of Japan have apparently been the ideal location.

Throughout Asia, the outdoor market mentality is widespread and constitutes a powerful element in its several national economies, not to mention in the everyday life of the people. A brief trip to Seoul's Itaewon district or to Petaling Jaya in Kuala Lumpur will give you the full flavour of this frenzied trade, and the wily bargain-hunter can usually ferret out anything from a pair of Reeboks to a Swiss army knife at a fraction of the normal price. Whether their goods are actually authentic or not is another matter.

Modern Japan, on the other hand, would appear by and large to have remained aloof from the nationwide outdoor selling culture promoted in the rest of Asia. Bona fide street markets, offering fashion merchandise and electrical products, certainly exist in larger cities such as Tokyo and Osaka, but venturing further afield you will be hard-pressed to find anything other than food related stalls and *yatai* (open-air night pubs). The average Japanese customer has come to expect the royal treatment as part of the excellent service provided by clean-cut retail outlets and he is more than willing to pay for it. This tendency has in recent times created a vacuum in the market and it comes as little surprise to discover that it is the Jews who have swarmed to fill it.

The Jews, often credited with being a people of enormous entrepreneurial expertise with a keen nose for scenting lucrative trades, particularly abroad, currently monopolise Japan's *gai-jin rotensho* or foreign street-business. Arriving in small numbers on tourist visas during the booming Eighties, most flocked to the large metropolitan areas of Honshu Island to ply their trade on any convenient street corner. As word spread and competition in the bigger cities grew fiercer, the new arrivals were forced to explore opportunities the full length of Japan. So, incidentally, were some of the weaker early pioneering urban sellers. After all, big money was at stake and it was survival of the fittest.

By the end of the Eighties, the main cities on even the rural islands of Hokkaido, Shikoku and Kyushu were occupied by resident sellers. They were incredibly territorial, believing in the unwritten law that being the first to sell in a city gave them ownership of the whole city, regardless of the fact that they invariably set up without asking anybody for permission. Even on the rare occasions when they paid protection money to the local *yakuza* or Japanese mafia, this in no way conferred upon them any legal right to sell on the street. However, with the fall of night in Japan, all manner of shady activities surface and the grey areas of the law seem to lurk hand in hand with them.

Year in and year out, the authorities have effectively closed their eyes to this primarily nocturnal foreign business activity. There has been the occasional localised raid by police on those selling fake brand-name goods, or, in co-ordination with local immigration, to capture those working on ninety-day sight-seeing visas. Nevertheless, the Israelis have modified their tricks accordingly.

The first sellers to arrive in Japan used to make a quick sortie to Korea at the expiry of their visa and re-enter at a different Japanese port where they would be issued with another three-month permit. Now they simply go abroad and conveniently lose their passports so that they can enter Japan afresh on a new one without all those telltale visitors' stamps to arouse immigration suspicions. Contractually arranged marriages are a common practice as with marriage comes the right of abode as well as the right to work, though, contrary to Israeli opinion, it does not bestow the right to set up shop in a public place on the street. For those who get deported, all that is required is a short trip to Bangkok with about $5,000. This apparently buys you a false passport and a new identity.

Initially, the foreigners peddled imported oil paintings from Thailand, but in the Nineties, most sellers have opted to deal in the more profitable business of costume jewellery. This is mainly imported from Korea, and it is far cheaper, infinitely easier to handle and produces a much faster turnover. In recent years, the Japanese too have finally entered the street business in large numbers, justifiably feeling entitled to a share of this multi-billion yen market on their own doorstep. The increased competition has seen a drop in profits for many and a proportional rise in tension, thus triggering widespread criminal activity.

However, the Japanese police seem reluctant to make a concerted nationwide effort to stamp out this illegal activity. Ham-fisted attempts to tackle it on a parochial level have merely displayed their professional ineptitude and hypocrisy as it emerges that they too are involved. The resultant cover-ups have revealed many inconsistencies not printed by newspaper editors because of a confederacy with the police. Now there is a growing minority who feel that there are questions to be answered and that the Japanese public has a right to know exactly what is going on in its towns and cities.

Background

It was in the winter of 1989, on the island of Kyushu, Japan, that I first became acquainted with the foreign street-selling industry. I had just taken up a teaching position on the Osumi peninsular of Kagoshima Prefecture, as part of the Japanese government's scheme to internationalise its schools and, more importantly, to promote the instruction of conversational English in the classrooms. Determined to master the Japanese language, as well as immerse myself in the culture, I would always go out on the town after working hours to indulge in the Kagoshima man's favourite pastime of *hashigo* which literally translates as 'ladder' but idiomatically signifies the art of the pub crawl.

This particular evening, I had ventured to the comparatively large city of Miakonojo for entertainment. In between bars, I was somewhat taken aback to come across a well-built Israeli selling pictures along a dimly-lit wall in the very centre of the nightlife area. Despite his rough appearance, he struck me as an amiable chap with infinitely better English than most of that which I had been exposed to in recent months. Apparently, he had been selling there for some time and was living in an old camper van with his girlfriend. While we talked, there was a great deal of passing interest in his stall, but few actually purchased anything. As I left for my third and final watering hole, I could not help feeling sorry for him.

My next encounter with an alien street trader came a year later after my move farther north on Kyushu to the much larger city of Kumamoto. I had signed up to work for the BBC Language School there and was relieved to have escaped from the confines of the Education Ministry's outmoded, grammar-oriented English teaching system. Not only did this city boast an exquisite Japanese garden and a majestic castle presiding over its population of half a million, but also a bustling nightlife area. With the after-dark temptations having increased tenfold and numerous newly-formed friendships, I embarked upon a social whirl, which effectively turned into a five-year drinking slalom. Consequently, I could not avoid meeting Budo.

The name itself was a contradiction in terms – he was a six-foot-plus, shaven-headed, fiercely proud, former Israeli policeman called 'Grape' which was what 'Budo' meant in Japanese. No wonder most of his customers sniggered cautiously when he introduced himself. Certainly, he was a sinister-looking individual with eyes like a hawk, as he hovered around his stall on Kumamoto's main arcade street, Shimotori. Many mistook him for a hoodlum, this alarming impression endorsed by his massive bear-like Israeli partner, Zak, who appeared every now and then, in between extended vacations in South-East Asia. This was their city and I could not see anyone trying to take it away from them.

Since the Kumamoto man's passion was no different from the Kagoshima man's passion, I spent the majority of my nights 'on the ladder' so to speak, flitting between *izakayas* (Japanese pubs) and *snaku* bars (hostess karaoke bars). Linguistically, it was incredibly instructive to converse in Japanese for so long in such relaxed surroundings, and the habit also enabled me to sample the atmospheres of a wide variety of the establishments in the city's *saka-riba* (drinking area). It also meant that during the course of an evening, I often used to stop and have a few words with Budo. He seemed to appreciate the visit as he would usually have long spells alone when nobody would stop to look at his oil paintings. I sometimes felt guilty that I was out having fun, while he was out shivering in the cold, confined to his own company. I could never do that, I told myself.

Budo had seemingly first come to Japan in 1988. He had tried his hand at selling in various locations all over the country, but had fallen in love with the slower pace of life and the friendliness of the people on Kyushu. This south lying island was at the time still virtually untouched by the Israeli street-selling invasion, so it was as much the lack of competition as more sentimental reasons that made him install himself as the regular *gai-jin* seller of Kumamoto, along with his part-time partner, of course. In those days, they were both perpetually operating on ninety-day tourist visas, though quite how Japanese immigration officials failed to clamp down on such conspicuous individuals, remains a mystery. After all, ten or more 'Temporary Visitor' stamps back-to-back in a passport had to be a bit of a give-away.

I got to know Budo only gradually over the years, because, by nature of his profession, he was very guarded. Naturally, he was also extremely street-wise because he had to know his way around the Japanese system for the practical side of his everyday existence. He could always advise you on where to get the cheapest used car, find the nearest second-hand shop or which airport you were least likely to be interrogated by immigration at. Underneath his frightening façade lay a sensitive, honest, upstanding character. However, linguistically and culturally, he remained an ignoramus in Japan. His lowly status as a street-seller excluded him from normal Japanese social circles, which relegated him and his kind to the periphery of society. His only Christmas party invitation would come from the boss of the local *yakuza*. Even acquiring a local wife did nothing to aid his integration into society – but it did give him a working visa, and with money his main goal, this was more important.

It was in the summer of 1994 that we became closer friends. Budo and Zak had fallen out, which was hardly surprising in a so-called partnership where one did all the work. The inevitable wrangling over money soon became violent as Budo was mercilessly beaten up twice on the street by his ex-partner. He did not retaliate because he had too much respect for the big man. His wide network of supposed friends, many of whom he had unselfishly helped in their street-selling businesses over the years, attempted to mediate but effectively deserted him in favour of Zak.

Since I was enjoying a six-week paid summer holiday from my college job at the time, I was free to act as a confidant to Budo for his ongoing saga. He was at an all-time low; totally depressed, completely lacking in confidence and with not the slightest desire to work. It took some weeks to break him out of this mood. In the process, I learnt a lot about the *basta* business (a Hebrew term used by Israelis to refer to their street shops) and became all the more curious about this different world with its potential for providing a more rounded insight into the Japanese. My interest in the whole street-selling racket prompted me during the spring of 1996 to get out onto the sidewalks and experience it for myself.

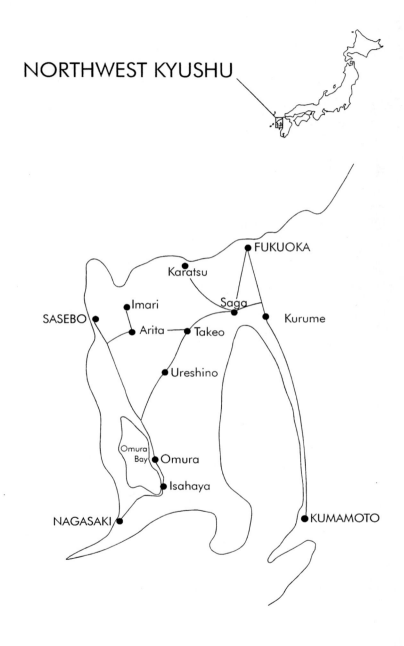

29th February, 1996

I climbed up into the van out of the pouring rain at around five o'clock. The faithful old Nissan Homy, Budo's constant companion through so many of his earlier street-selling adventures, coughed and spluttered into life, the noisy diesel engine shattering the serenity of his country home. I crunched the unfamiliar gears into reverse, backed up to face the road, and then pulled away as my Jewish friend shouted, 'Good luck.'

It had taken most of the day to prepare my *basta,* which consisted mainly of Budo's jewellery accessories, plus a substantial number of goods that I had carried over from England, such as sports shirts and a variety of tourist-type souvenirs. This was now all loaded behind the driver's seat, extending under the elevated horizontal sheet of plywood which constituted a bed-board for my futon. For the next couple of months, this ageing minibus, stripped of its rear passenger seats, was to be my business office, storeroom, and my home.

Progress was slow along Kumamoto's Higashi By-pass. It was rush-hour and the vehicles were nose to tail. Once I finally got onto the Kyushu Expressway heading north to Fukuoka, I was able to put my foot down and I felt a little more relaxed. Although I had spent the best part of seven years in Japan, and had come to regard it almost as a second home, today marked a new dimension to my existence here. Whilst half of me felt stimulated by the prospect of this fresh experience, and the alternative view it would undoubtedly offer me of my host nation, the other half felt ashamed to be entering into a trade to which so much stigma was evidently attached. After all, I had been the revered *sensei* up until now, literally meaning 'first born', or 'teacher' in common parlance.

The *sensei* in Japan is accorded a kind of awesome respect, regardless of whether he deserves it or not. During Japan's rapid industrial and technological development in the second half of this century, with so few resident native English teachers, just about any long-nosed, fair-complexioned foreigner who turned up on his boat or aircraft would be accorded *sensei* status. A perfect example lay in the infamous Bulgarian of Kumamoto City who had arrived on these shores in the early Seventies with barely a word of English, took on the title of 'University Professor', and proceeded to learn the language at the same time as he taught his students. In recent years, a large influx of qualified foreigners has indeed raised the educational standards, but there are still a surprising number of so-called native English teachers, (with useful degrees in subjects like plant biology), who do not know the first thing about language instruction.

The Israeli street-seller in Japan on the other hand, automatically regarded as to all intents and purposes a social outcast here, ironically enough is often far more intelligent, much better travelled, has superior English and an infinitely greater experience of life than his local detractors. However, in a country where image is so important, he is invariably treated like scum, and not attributed with an ounce of intelligence. I had often thought that this made a mockery of Japan's much-hyped 'classless society', to which supposedly, everyone's particular contribution is valued, whether manual or cerebral.

As I turned west to join the motorway for Nagasaki, I continued my ruminations on social status and how we are regarded by others. I remembered a quotation from Shakespeare that seemed very apt: 'Reputation is an idle and most false imposition; oft got without merit and lost without deserving.'

This speech of Iago's from *Othello* then provoked more worrying thoughts on a personal level. What if my Japanese friends found out about my new venture? How would they regard me and would their knowledge of my street-selling affect our relationship negatively? I suspected that it would, because even though out of respect to me, most of them had been superficially friendly towards Budo over the years, none of them really wanted anything to do with him on a deeper level. Their tacit disparagement, combined with my own sense of pride, had forced me to keep this latest activity a secret from everybody except Budo. I just prayed that the places I was destined to sell in would be sufficiently distant and obscure as to prevent any embarrassing chance encounters.

Towards ten past seven, I saw the sign for Omura and decided to leave the expressway. I knew from Budo's explanations that this small city's only nightlife area pitch was exposed, so I would have to work in the sheltered position of the pub-building in Isahaya City. There was a national road linking them up and it was no more than twelve kilometres between the two. Isahaya and Omura City were, according to Budo and his version of Israeli street-selling law, his by right because he had verbally inherited them from another Jewish street-seller who had since returned to Tel Aviv. He had also apparently worked here during his early days in Japan, and had more recently employed various individuals to sell for him here on a typical thirty-five per cent commission basis. I however, being a close friend of Budo's, had arranged to keep seventy per cent of any jewellery sales, whilst the remainder would go to him to cover the cost of the merchandise and expenses for the van. The profits from my British goods were to be entirely mine.

After stopping for a quick bite to eat at one of the numerous twenty-four-hour shops along the way, I finished the journey to Isahaya and, thanks to Budo's foolproof map, located the imposing nightlife building. It was called Dai San Royal Building and consisted of at least eight floors. The ground floor was spacious and open, with five brightly-lit doors at its perimeter leading to various drinking establishments. At the centre was a tiled, concrete platform and behind this, the lift. Because of the building's open quadrangular design, which allowed one to look down from the ascending balconies, there was fine netting draped across the space, to catch any falling objects that might prove hazardous to people below. As I got my bearings, a few *snaku* bar hostesses arrived for their evening shifts, smelling freshly bathed and lightly perfumed. It reminded me of my Kumamoto football team and the goalkeeper's wedding parties that I had attended the previous Sunday – a world away from the business I was about to embark upon.

I set up my stall around the concrete platform. First I slotted three sets of plywood trestles together. These were the legs for the cloth-covered boards which I then laid on top, upon which to display the costume jewellery cases and my articles from Britain. Beside this I erected another wooden case in which hung a comprehensive range of necklaces, and that was basically all there was to it – a simple rough-and-ready portable shop which was made to look really quite presentable in no more than ten minutes. I knew that in the right place it could yield countless millions of yen, just as many stalls of its type had done over the years up and down the country. Mind you, on a cold, rainy evening in a quiet building at the heart of rural Nagasaki, I had no such illusions.

After four hours of shivering, with only one female customer to show for it, I declared the evening a wash-out, packed up and drove off to the nearby park, resolving to start in earnest with the arrival of the new month the following day. I washed in the public conveniences before stepping up into my new bedroom and shutting the dismal day out with a certain feeling of reclusive satisfaction. But I was somewhat disappointed to have made a mere Y4,000 (£25) start to my street-selling adventure.

1st March

I awoke the next morning to the sound of voices and banging car doors. It took a few moments for me to register where I was, and the sight of my own breath confirmed that I was not dreaming. My bed was actually very snug and I was glad that I had decided to throw in an extra blanket as, contrary to popular belief, Kyushu's early morning pre-spring temperatures do not differ greatly to those of London. I was also relieved that I had had the good sense to install some makeshift curtains because the role of goldfish at this hour was not particularly appealing.

Sitting up on my elbows, I cracked open a can of cold 'Boss' coffee, tucked into a currant bun, and started to ponder upon my new situation.

Financially speaking, I was in the red. The previous evening's anti-climax did not even cover the expressway toll, let alone the fuel for the van. However, the up side was that my time was my own and I didn't have to answer to anybody except myself. Also, today was Friday, which for anyone connected with the retail business in Japan, always signalled the start of the weekend's hectic trade. So it was on this note of optimism that I got up in a leisurely way, washed in the park's public facilities and set off on walkabout to orientate myself in my local surroundings.

Within an hour, I had managed to locate everything I needed to provide me with a comfortable level of existence, and this included amongst other things a *sentou* and a selection of *kissaten*. The former is basically a simple bathhouse, which is the cheaper, less luxurious version of the more widely recognised *onsen* or hot-spring bath, but in my experience, there was sometimes little to choose between them. The *kissaten* is Japan's equivalent to the coffee shop, where, during the week, a very competitively-priced and healthy *hi-gawari teishoku* or set lunch is served between the hours of 11.30 a.m. and 2 p.m. This type of establishment is an excellent place to escape from the world for half an hour or so (except perhaps during the above times), and is often frequented by lone males absorbed in their adult comics or *manga*. In fact, even when on a date, many a Japanese male has been known to immerse himself in his book, leaving his lady to chat to her glass of water.

After a spot of lunch, I set off back to the van, stopping at a public telephone box on the way to listen to the day's local weather forecast. On hearing that it was nought per cent rain for Nagasaki Prefecture, I headed off for the little city of Omura in search of its night-time selling spot out in the open. This proved, surprisingly, a little more difficult to find, probably because I followed signs to the station which did not take me through the main city centre. However, directions from a kind, sun-tanned man eventually led me to a newly pink-paved street called *Renga-Doori* or Brick Street. It was deserted except for two beer-delivery vans. These, the mass of *snaku* bars lining either side of the road, and the low white wall Budo had mentioned, told me that I had found Omura's *saka-riba*. Now I could go and find a *sentou* to relax in all afternoon.

★

I set up my stall in front of the little white wall shortly before eight o'clock. The sky was clear, revealing its mighty constellations, but with no cloud cover, there was a fair nip in the air. Brick Street was alive with a buzz of anticipation. Liquor shop employees were scurrying to make last minute deliveries while hostesses in their short skirts and high heels hopped out of their boyfriends' cars to clack noisily into their alcohol-soaked lairs. One, a stumpy girl called Miyuki, with black boots up to her thighs, came to buy a soft drink at the vending machine next to my stall. We talked for a while before she gave a big business smile and trotted back to the 'Embassy', which was apparently the name of her *snaku*. I couldn't help thinking that, had I been Israeli instead of a reticent Englishman, I would have arranged for her to give me a personal guided tour of the town later on that night.

Things were pretty slow at first, but as the night wore on and the customers left their warm *izakayas* to get into their *snaku*-bar-hopping modes, the street became ever livelier. By 11 p.m. the drinking street was packed with groups of Japanese men arguing about which should be the next rung on the drinking ladder. The two fundamental criteria dictating their next port of call were always beautiful young hostesses, and a pre-paid for bottle of spirits kept to one side with their name on it. This was a game with which I was all too familiar, yet it seemed somehow strange now to be on the outside looking in. I felt the isolation any non-drinker must surely experience when surrounded by inebriates, and I could partially understand Budo's mercenary comment about patronising drunkards:

'They come along to my *basta* with full wallets and young air-heads on their arms. As long as they can inflate themselves at my expense with a token word of slurred English and a few condescending jabs at my lowly position, they are soon willing to part with Y5,000 (£30), before laughing at me and leaving. Little do they know that the bracelet they have just bought cost me Y100 in Korea. Then I am the one who is laughing – in my pocket!'

At one stage, two tall Americans passed in front of my shop, but they looked in every other possible direction so as to avoid saying 'hello'. I had never been an advocate of going out of your way to speak to fellow *gai-jin* in Japan, but in a street twelve feet wide in the middle of nowhere, it seemed a bit unsociable not to. Again, I could not help recalling Budo, who was amazingly sensitive about being snubbed by foreigners – and that was in Kumamoto's Shimotori Street, which had to be at least three times the width of Brick Street. He would always bitterly refer to them as 'f—ing condescending English teachers', and if he didn't get the opportunity to embarrass them directly for having ignored him, he would content himself with telling me that his earnings were on average five times what theirs were.

I sold steadily until the early hours of the morning and thoroughly enjoyed myself in the process. It was exhilarating to share views and quick-fire repartee with a cross-section of people and get paid for it. In the past in Japan, I had had to get drunk with the people to have these types of conversations, and at the end of the night, had paid an arm and a leg for the privilege. On the whole, it was those in groups who were the boldest, the most talkative and sometimes the most obnoxious as they tried to impress their peers. But the best comment of the night came from a solitary man in his mid-forties on the subject of Japan's *mizu-shoubai*, literally translated as 'water business', but figuratively referring to all forms of nightlife enterprises.

'When I was younger,' he said, 'I used to be a sad, lonely sod spending all my salary in *snakus* and clubs, thinking the hostesses really liked me as opposed to just humouring me because they were being paid to do so. No, I don't go to that kind of place any more. In fact, it's changed my life – now I'm a sad, lonely sod with money.'

2nd March

Whereas during weekdays most street-sellers would not ordinarily work before dark due to a lack of places in which to set up shop, weekends are holidays for many non-retail institutions such as banks and post offices thus offering perfect pitches for such traders to work at around the clock. Unlike in Kumamoto, Isahaya and Omura's shopping areas did not intersect conveniently with their nightlife areas, so the daytime pitch was in a different place from the night-time pitch. Therefore, the previous afternoon I had walked up and down Isahaya's long arcade hunting for a suitable spot for my shop the following morning, as well as for a couple of options for parking.

I rose early that Saturday morning, and after splashing my face with ice-cold water in the toilets of the nearby park, I set off with that slight feeling of tense anticipation that one often experiences when starting something new in a new place. To be honest, part of the uneasiness was definitely due to my knowing that the business activity in which I was engaged had not actually received the Emperor's seal of approval, so to speak. I drew up in front of Isahaya's Number 18 Bank, which, as I had expected, was closed. It was in an ideal location at the heart of the arcade. As I unloaded my trestles, boards and merchandise, I noticed that a suited man in his sixties was staring at me with disapproval from the front of his gift shop twenty metres further down the street. I pretended to ignore him, but could not help worrying that he might complain to the local authorities about my presence. It was with this on my mind that I temporarily abandoned my things to go and park the van for free, five hundred yards away by the river. I returned at a jog some eight minutes later, relieved to find everything just as I had left it, and began to set up, admiring, not for the first time, the apparent lack of criminality in Japan.

Although this was only my third day of selling, I was mildly concerned that nobody had shown much interest in the range of football and rugby shirts that I had brought over from London. Because of this, I devoted at least fifteen minutes to displaying an eye-catching sample of them as attractively as I could, and made them a priority item in my sales patter. There were already at this early hour of eleven o'clock, a lot of passing youngsters so I had high hopes of a successful session. I knew from Budo's working routine that weekends usually marked the peak in takings because many of the Japanese had days off and often went out for a bit of family shopping.

For the first hour I felt like a leper, as nobody would stop and I certainly was not the thick-skinned type to bawl at the top of my voice, forcing people to give me their attention. I happily greeted anyone who passed close by with a friendly *Konnichiwa* ('Hello!') or *Irashaimase* ('Welcome'), otherwise, I would just stand and wait. This in itself, I discovered, was rather intimidating for the Japanese, who are as a race shy at the best of times, their confidence waning even more when confronted by a foreigner. Therefore, I decided to use the tactic of pretending to be a customer, instead of standing erect behind the stall waiting to pounce. I feigned concentrated rearrangement of my display cases, and within a few minutes, I would invariably be joined by browsers, who would in turn attract more browsers, and before I knew it, there would be a real crowd. I later learnt that this phenomenon in Japan was known as *sakura* literally translated as 'cherry blossom', but used to signify the sudden blooming of many around the first open bud.

I did my best to have a few words with each customer to make them feel relaxed and to strike up a natural, light-hearted conversation when possible about anything other than the goods on my stall. Making them laugh was all important and fortunately, my seven years on the *hashigo* had furnished me with a number of the key clichés. It was a little bit like performing on a stage; in fact, at times I felt that I derived far more satisfaction from the human contact and the entertaining than I did from selling. If the customer had obviously come to practise his English, I would reluctantly oblige by switching to my own language, but it reminded me too much of the tedium of the classroom. Linguistically, I was a firm advocate of the 'When in Rome...' philosophy, believing that when abroad you should always try to speak the language of that country, unless, that is, you would be insulting the indigenous listener due to his greater fluency in your own language.

I had taken about Y11,000 (£60) by lunchtime. Feeling a bit peckish, I put some coloured cloth sheets over my ring cases and crossed the road to Daiei supermarket, where I went down to the basement to purchase a *bentou* (Japanese-style boxed lunch) along with a carton of milk. I then quickly hurried back to my shop to consume the goodies in great haste behind my boards, because I was well aware that only real plebs dare to eat in public in this country. The *bentou* was excellent with its full range of vitamins, though the Japanese milk, as usual, left a lot to be desired.

From two o'clock to four o'clock that afternoon, business improved. A lot of students were returning home after their school club activities, and there were a lot of couples out on the street. I couldn't help noticing that some of the younger ones were even quite openly walking hand in hand, a rare occurrence back in the 1980s. In Japan, apparently, public displays of affection had always been frowned upon so perhaps this traditionally emotionally undemonstrative race was indeed changing, I thought to myself.

I spent half an hour joking with a group of junior high school girls who were trying to persuade me to give them a ring each for Y100 (60 pence). The normal price was actually Y500, but they were so cute that I gave them all a London key-ring for nothing. They left happily, only to return twenty minutes later with a cake for me which I found very touching. They also gave me a tiny sticker photo each of their impish little faces, telling me that they had just had a whole sheet of these minute pictures taken in a nearby booth. Apparently, it was one of the latest crazes in Japan.

By half past four, I was fairly tired, and knowing I was in for a long night, I decided to close up and head off to the old *sentou* straight down the road. As luck would have it, it was closed, so I had to use the bath-house and sauna facilities of a neighbouring business hotel that turned out to be four times the price. I strongly begrudged this extra expense, not because I couldn't afford it, but because the object of this way of life was to live as frugally as possible. After all, I had come in search of an authentic street-selling experience and not one that would be tainted by luxury – mind you, it was still early days.

*

With the thought of the very respectable profits of the previous evening still imprinted on my mind, it was with a certain amount of enthusiasm that I set up my stall in front of the low white wall in Omura's Brick Street. The early part of the evening was quiet, except for the noisy arrival of the traffic police demanding that everyone who had parked their vehicles in the nearby deserted shopping arcade should move them immediately. This included me, and it was with some trepidation that I scampered over to remove my van. I was totally sycophantic as I humbly apologised for my misdeed and then commended the honourable policeman on his great skill at English, despite its being completely unintelligible. Anyway, it paid off, because after I'd answered a few questions and shown my Japanese driving licence, they allowed me to go, without even referring to my job on the street. I took this as tacit permission to continue.

To my enquiry as to where might be a good place to leave the van, the senior policeman replied, 'Well, we cannot touch you, if you leave it in the car park of the disused theatre, a little bit further down on the left.'

Thanking them profusely, I went to do just that, smiling at the policeman's tendency to shift responsibility, and the typical Japanese reluctance to make a definite statement. I also could not help wondering quite who would touch me.

Back at my stall, at about quarter to ten, a man with closely cropped grey hair stopped and chatted pleasantly with me for a while before purchasing a lighter. I guessed that he was around retirement age but he looked in very good shape for his years. He was debating whether to buy something else when a group of men in suits approached, the tallest one yelling out in my direction, 'O-mae wa mada daijoobu ka?' ('Are you still all right?')

The word *O-mae* meaning 'you' is often used towards inferiors and is exceedingly insulting, not to mention confrontational, when directed at strangers. I was angry inside, but fought to keep my cool, realising, as most sellers with an ounce of intelligence do, that the name of this game is non-confrontation, if you are to keep making hay while the Japanese sun shines. Any trouble would merely put the foreigner in the spotlight and jeopardise his early retirement plans.

I responded by mimicking his question, but pointedly used the formal version of the personal pronoun and the verb to let him know that he was not addressing a complete imbecile, 'O-taku wa mada daijoobu desu ka?'

My customer, on the other hand, was incensed by the sudden interruption, and by such blatant rudeness towards me. He instantly squared up to the taller man, 'Who the hell are you to break in and be so offensive?'

'Immigration,' came the simple reply in English.

This confirmed my suspicion that his crudely put question had not merely been an enquiry after my health, but was a reference to the fact that a foreigner was still selling here and had not yet been carted off by the authorities. I was in absolutely no doubt about his authenticity, since such a technical word does not simply roll off the tongue of your average English-speaking Japanese. Naturally, the kind old man wasn't quite aware of this subtlety and all its implications. He could only register that the previous harmony existing between us had been destroyed by a younger, apparently obnoxious individual and he was not having any of it, especially after a drop of sake.

I shrank into the background as the old man gave him a torrent of verbal abuse and then moved threateningly towards the immigration officer, who was also ready for a spot of fisticuffs until his marginally more sober colleagues dragged him away. He took some persuading, but in the end went off reluctantly. I was left with a feeling of foreboding, but I was genuinely touched by the old man's protective instinct towards me. I thanked him for his defensive efforts and told him not to worry about it because I was accustomed to that sort of treatment. This was an absolute lie – I was seething.

Within half an hour the police drew up. I was aware of their patrol car just as I was taking some money for a ring. I furtively pocketed the notes when the two officers approached. The more senior one took charge and very courteously went through the preliminary formalities of looking at my passport and my driving licence, writing details of both in a notebook. That done, he apologetically informed me that they had received a call from a member of the public that they were obliged to act upon, and that consequently they must ask me if I would possibly mind moving on to find an alternative spot.

He bravely tried to use a few words of English, which to his great delight I complimented him upon, although I opted to use Japanese so that I would be seen to be co-operating and so that they would understand perfectly what I was saying. I stuck to the story that I was travelling and was just selling to put food in my mouth. The older one appeared sympathetic, apologising once more for having no choice but to obey orders, while the younger one, I sensed, would dearly love to have put me through the wringer had he not been under the direction of his superior.

I told them that I fully understood their position, apologised obsequiously for what I had done, packed up my things and shot off to sell in Isahaya, cursing the tall turd from immigration all the way.

3rd March

Having sold moderately successfully in the building until half past two in the morning, making it a thirteen hour working day, it was with some effort that I forced myself out of bed at nine o'clock the following morning. However, knowing that I was going to take that night off, as according to Budo Sunday nights in the small cities were usually 'crappy', made things a little easier.

My first two hours in front of Number 18 Bank were again fairly quiet. I was once more aware of the disgruntled looks from the elderly man in the gift shop, but I ignored him, and after setting up, settled down for a quiet period of contemplation with my Japanese proverb book. I had positioned my chair a little bit back from my shop in order to catch the rising sun as it filtered through the partially covered arcade roof, and for the first time since commencing this outdoor trade, I actually felt warm.

Up until lunchtime, I was not exactly rushed off my feet, but there was a steady flow of window shoppers. Whereas the majority of my customers at night were male, in the daytime, for the most part, they were female or children. Consequently, except for one or two boisterous junior high school students, this was the more reserved, more civilised part of the day, whilst the evening consumption of alcohol tended to bring out a bolder more bumptious side of the Japanese character. The opening lines from the customer, however, never varied much, regardless of whether one was a foreign teacher or a foreign street-seller:

'Wow, your Japanese is good!' when you have just said, 'Hello'.

'How long have you been here to speak that well?' when you've correctly remembered your own name.

'Seven years! Only seven years in the country and you are already that fluent. You must be brave to come all this way on your own, as well as clever to have mastered our very difficult language in that time. We Japanese could never do that. We learn English for six years in high school and junior high school and come out unable even to say, "This is a pen" without making a mistake. Anyway, whereabouts in America are you from?'

You try to keep smiling and ignore such a flagrant insult.

'London, you say? That's a trendy place but it's always shrouded in fog, isn't it?'

You explain that even though Charles Dickens' London, with all its industrial and residential chimney smoke, did give that impression, things really have improved a lot since then.

'Ah, soo nan desu ka?' would come the totally unconvinced reply.

'Anyway, I want to go and do a homestay in America to learn real English.'

You resist the temptation to ask why on earth they would want to go there with such a pointless objective, but decide to wish them all the best instead.

That day certainly saw its fair share of similar conversations and it was with some relief that I closed my shop towards five o'clock. I bought a few cans of beer at the local off-licence, where the woman on the till obligingly exchanged my wallet-full of smaller notes for a couple of the larger denomination variety, before retiring to the seclusion of my van to count my takings. Altogether so far, I had slightly under Y111,000. Although compared to bigger cities such as Kumamoto – where Budo would often make that in just a Saturday – it was disappointing, for smaller cities such as Isahaya and Omura, it really was quite respectable for half a week's work, and definitely exceeded what I could earn as an English teacher.

With this satisfying thought in mind, I drove back along the congested national route to Omura and its huge sauna-*onsen* complex, known as Kuwa-Kuwa. It was here that I stayed all night, totally indulging myself in the numerous baths of varying temperatures, in the culinary delights of the restaurant-bar, and in the entertainment provided by the multi-screen television room. What a contrast to the old *sentous*, I thought, where you had to take your own soap and towel. Here, everything was laid on, right down to pyjamas and cotton buds, not to mention the resident masseuses. I suddenly felt like a king, which is exactly how the Japanese expect to feel when they are paying handsomely for it. In the luxury of my palace, I forgot all about my lust for an authentic street-selling experience.

6th March

Another rainy night the following Wednesday dictated that I open in the shelter of Dai San Royal Building, as opposed to Omura's exposed spot on Brick Street. This was slightly annoying as the building gave me a trapped, claustrophobic sort of feeling, whilst out in the fresh air I felt jubilantly unconstrained. There were two other reasons why I did not particularly like this indoor place; the ground floor *snaku* called 'Spur', to the left of me, had an unusually pretentious Mama san and the next door bar was the local bikers' hangout called 'Gangsters'.

Early on in the evening, the familiar cry of, 'Luke! Nan ba sho do?' signalled the moment I had most been dreading. Before even looking up, I knew from the dialectal tones that I had been discovered by someone from my former life in Kumamoto and, sure enough, there was my ex-football team's left-winger, Takasaki san. He looked as embarrassed as I felt. I tried to remain natural as I explained that I was just giving Budo a hand for a few days because I had nothing better to do, and immediately changed the subject to the goalkeeper's wedding that we had both attended a fortnight previously. He in turn explained that his company, Honda, had transferred him to Isahaya, but that he did not like it much because he had not yet managed to make any friends. This was apparently the reason he frequented *snaku* bars alone at night; to get a little companionship. We talked for a while before he went on his way to his regular hostess joint. It seemed that he was sniggering at me as we parted, though perhaps I was just being paranoid.

Still dwelling on the fact that I had been found out so early into the game, I suddenly noticed that there was a glaring empty space in my sports shirt section – one of my display rugby shirts had been stolen from right under my nose. I racked my brains to recall the groups that had passed during my conversation with Takasaki. As far as I could remember, only two young men had stopped, but I had not noticed them touching anything. I was livid and first of all raced out to the front of the building to see if anyone was hurrying away, but there was no one. Next, I scoured the above balconies for any clues; however, I found nothing. It was not until twenty minutes later, when I decided to check out the emergency stairs, that I detected the shirt's pink metal hanger discarded half-way up. This at least confirmed that I was not suffering from premature senility, but it did not get me any nearer to finding the culprit.

The night had not started well and I was in a disconsolate mood until the president of a company stopped by with his friend, jokingly put five of my brashest imitation rings on to each one of his right hand's fat fingers, and produced the appropriate payment with a hearty laugh. I had to smile. My smile later turned into a grin as a young man came along and purchased a Liverpool football shirt, as well as a rugby shirt, both at eight times the price I had paid for them in London. I hardly needed a calculator to work out that these sales more than compensated for the earlier theft, though it still irritated me to think that I had been robbed, especially in broad night-light, so to speak.

The final treat on this eventful night came as I was talking to one of the bikers from the Gangster bar. He came to the building every night and was apparently part of the management team, though by all accounts, there was a distinct lack of customers at the bar, which according to him – and to some others I had spoken to – would very soon lead to its closure. As I went through the motions of sympathising with his plight, a drunk young *snaku* bar hostess walked by with her giant of a boyfriend. She obviously knew the biker because she virtually yelped in ecstasy as she greeted him. He leered after her and exclaimed in a loud voice that he could see she was wearing nothing but a 'T-back' (G-string panties) under her light, see-through mini-skirt. With that, the hostess bent forward, lifting the back of her skirt with one hand and peeling away the T-back with the other to reveal her shocking clitoris. Her boyfriend, thankfully, strode on in total oblivion.

After packing away my things at about 2.30 a.m., I had a quick drink in Gangsters, as promised, with the young man who had bought the shirts. Then I got into the van and headed off back towards Omura. Conscious of the bad weather forecast, as much as wanting to avoid any further moral corruption in Isahaya's building, I made the spontaneous decision to explore further afield. I had heard from Budo that there was another sheltered opening place in a town called Ureshino, in the neighbouring prefecture of Saga, so seeing as I was still wide-awake and there was little traffic on the road at this hour, I decided to continue in that direction.

7th March

The spa town of Ureshino at lunchtime was like a ghost town. I parked the van at a supermarket and wandered along the main street hunting for a place to eat. Being a prime tourist spot (or so I had read), it had plenty of hotels and souvenir shops, but seemingly a distinct lack of the faithful old *kissaten* that I had come to rely upon for my dish of the day.

I entered a large, modern-looking building called 'Happy Town', which was somewhat paradoxical seeing as the atmosphere was as silent and gloomy as the grave. It consisted of a narrow alleyway straddled by *snaku* and *yakitori* (grilled chicken) bars. They were all shuttered up, their apparent daytime abandonment no doubt belying their frantic evening trade. An old lady with brown-rinsed hair emerged from the darkness. She was laden with shopping but managed a friendly smile. I asked her if she knew of a coffee shop in the vicinity where I might get a bite to eat. She did, and urged me to follow her because it was on her way home.

She led me out the other side of Happy Town, which was evidently a regular short-cut for her, down a steep flight of stone steps towards the river, and along a narrow path that ran parallel to its bank. I commented on there not being a soul in sight and was informed that it was typical for this hour of the day. She assured me that by early evening I would witness a complete transformation as bus-loads of sightseers would overnight at the numerous *onsen* hotels before carrying on their way to the bigger cities like Nagasaki the next morning.

I was suddenly struck by her total trust and absence of fear, considering that I was a young male stranger, and a foreigner to boot. What a pleasant contrast to the increasing wariness required by women, young and old, in similar situations in England if they are to avoid being raped or bludgeoned to death down quiet paths such as this.

We continued to exchange the usual pleasantries, during the course of which we nimbly crossed the river by a series of stepping stones that I guessed would have severely tested someone twenty years her junior in my own country. Once on the other side, she pointed me in the direction of a small restaurant, wished me good luck and was on her way. It was not until the moment of our parting that she revealed her eighty-three years, leaving me merely to marvel at yet another fine example of the plucky Japanese octogenarian spirit.

★

After a hearty meal followed by a relaxing bath I was ready for a nap, because my sleep in the truckers' lay-by earlier that morning could only be described as fitful. There was no need for a reconnaissance mission to search for that night's selling spot as there was only one small drinking area, and I had already pin-pointed the best position thanks to another useful Budo landmark.

I slept soundly until seven o'clock. It was dark by then but the late night supermarket where I was parked seemed to be doing a roaring trade. I sat up on my futon and made myself a primitive sandwich of dry bread with a slice of processed cheese. Despite a craving for beer, I settled instead for a can of cold coffee. As usual, I felt slightly apprehensive, not sure what the night held in store for me.

I set up an hour later next to the entrance of a *snaku*, in a tiny building opposite Ureshino's main tourist hotel. As soon as I arrived, the Mama san came out to give me the once over and it took only the mention of Budo's name to enlist her as a friend for life. She altruistically treated each of her two young part-time workers to a set of earrings, and I gave her a hefty discount to complete our mutual expression of good will. Almost immediately she proved instrumental in preventing my immediate shut-down when an authoritarian little bureaucrat insisted that my presence would definitely lead to trouble, and that I should go to sell elsewhere. The kindly Mama san, with all her years of sympathetic diplomacy, pointed to the impeccable track record of problem-free foreign stalls outside her *snaku*, in an effort to pacify him. Eventually, he conceded that I could remain open for just a few hours in order not to totally lose face to the forceful Mama san, but we all knew that he would not be coming back to check later on. Relieved at not having been cut off in my prime, I presented the next passing little girl with a colourful silk bracelet. She gave me a delighted smile and, after prompting from her toothpick-chewing father, screamed, 'Arigatou gozaimashita.' The Mama san then whispered to me that I had just honoured the big boss of the local *yakuza*.

The morning's sprightly old lady was right. Ureshino, by night, was bursting with life. The hotel car parks were full and the drinking area was a mass of *yukata*-clad beings clomping up and down the streets in their ethnic *geta* (Japanese-style clogs), as they searched for their place of nocturnal entertainment. Many of the sightseers found it quite a novel idea to return to their respective homes after a trip to Nagasaki bearing souvenirs from London. Though I did not make a financial killing, I did manage to get rid of a large quantity of thitherto unpopular Queen's Guard magnets.

11th March

The Takeo public spa was excellent value at Y260 a dip, and was a spacious *onsen* affording plenty of room, not only around the baths, but inside as well – a much appreciated luxury during the chock-a-block early evening rush hour, when a lethargic stretch in the wrong direction could leave you with a lot of explaining to do.

It was the middle of the afternoon, so it was still relatively quiet with no more than a handful of bodies in evidence. These mostly belonged to elderly men who seemed to be very much in their element, lounging around on the cool slab-stones outside the tubs with all the nonchalance of tourists on Waikiki beach. Whilst they seemed totally unconcerned about freely exposing their withered piles, an almost extravagant modesty protected their front regions by way of a strategically placed towel, or in many cases, a clenched fist reminiscent of Greece's tragic Dikaiopolis during his moments of great anxiety.

As I was relaxing in one of the two larger baths, attempting to decipher the long list of rules and regulations hand-written in Chinese characters on a board attached to the wall, I got talking to a mild-mannered man called Mr Ikeda – or rather, he got talking to me. Apparently, he was a pottery expert, as well as a part-time English teacher, from the small neighbouring city of Imari. Too ashamed to admit the true purpose of my visit here, I gave an evasively economical version of reality. This certainly was far easier to achieve through the medium of my own language which Ikeda san had seemed intent on using from the start. Experience had shown me that I was a poor liar even under normal circumstances, and the added constraints imposed by a foreign tongue would render me worse than hopeless.

Our bathing companions gradually grew in number as Ikeda san made it his business to find out all about me and then proceeded to give an automatic translation of our entire conversation to the curious onlookers. Where he hadn't quite understood or where my answers were briefly uninformative, he would allow himself a touch of artistic licence. An example of this lay in my citing an interest in pottery as the prime purpose of my visit here. A little Ikeda embroidery inflated my status to the representative of a leading British ceramic company on a buying mission. Perhaps we had something in common after all.

We were chatting about various subjects when, out of the blue, he enquired, 'Have you heard of the Penis religion?'

His pronunciation of the vital word was a bit off, as in 'pen', so I had to make sure that I had understood him correctly, which I had.

'No, I can't say I have,' I replied, trying to keep a straight face.

'Well,' he continued in all seriousness, 'it's a widely followed religion in this area.'

'Umm, very appropriate, too,' I commented with a quick grin and a sweeping glance at all the protruding objects around us. Mr Ikeda's poker-faced expression made me chastise myself for such glibness and add yet another attempted sarcastic witticism to the 'fell as flat as a pancake in Japan' consignment, which was eventually destined for Britain, no doubt only to be sent straight back again.

Ikeda san went on to explain that there was a large phallic monument in the vicinity and that it represented the centre of worship for the followers of this religion. Its creed was apparently based on purity and health, with a heavy emphasis on the field of procreation – the birth of *genki* babies, that is to say those who are completely free of sickness. He offered to take me to the monument, but I politely declined, thinking that I had seen more than my fair share of genitals for one day.

We continued to chat idly for a while before I made my excuses and bade him farewell, as the hot bath was beginning to overwhelm me. I towelled myself down and dressed lazily, the hot water having sapped all my energy. Just as I was climbing into the van, Ikeda san emerged brandishing his business card, along with a handful of Imari pottery pamphlets in English. I in turn handed him my London card, thanked him profusely, and bowed in equal proportions, simultaneously praying that he wouldn't see me selling on the street at some later stage.

★

The weather forecast predicted twenty per cent rain for Saga Prefecture, so having decided to take a chance on the uncovered pitch offered by Takeo's small drinking area, I was left to hope that this city was situated in the eighty per cent sector. With only one main building of any significance in the *saka-riba*, the site for my stall was effectively predetermined. I had no information from Budo because he couldn't even remember having sold here. My initial impression during my post-bath reconnaissance mission, however, was not one of optimism, since there was not a single soul in sight, let alone a beer delivery van.

As darkness fell and the clock ticked laboriously round to half past seven, I cat-napped in the back of the Nissan, which I had parked in the anonymity of a supermarket parking area just outside Takeo. After rousing myself, I quickly popped out to purchase a stock of cut-price cans of coffee and a packet of buns past its sell-by date for my breakfasts. I then set off for work, impressed by my own tightfistedness.

The drinking street was just as I had left it, except for a burly individual in a black leather coat patrolling the shadowy path in front of a dimly lit building about fifty yards further down. Putting aside my heightened scepticism as to the wisdom of the evening's mission, and ignoring the ominous looks being shot in my direction, I speedily unloaded my things before shooting off to park the van behind a nearby convenience store. I returned at a run to find everything just as it had been and proceeded to set out my stall along the front wall of the modern two-storey building.

Within a few minutes, a woman in an apron emerged from the *yakitori* bar on the right of the stairs. Her shop was actually the first thing I had noticed when perusing the building that afternoon because this was my favourite type of Japanese *izakaya*. It was typified by its red lantern hanging over a door that undoubtedly led to a cosy counter area with a wide variety of skewered meats on display, ready to be grilled by the master in front of you. She examined my merchandise with a trained eye, asked me a few prices, and then wished me better luck than she'd been having that night, before disappearing back into her shop.

Two minutes later, the master of the next but one *raamen* (Chinese noodle) shop stopped by with a bowl of steaming pork noodles on his way to make a delivery by bicycle. 'Thought you looked a bit cold out here. Anyway, get this down you and I'll pick the bowl up on the way back,' he said.

'Doumo arigatou gozaimashita,' I replied somewhat inadequately and gulped them down gratefully. I was joined in mid-slurp by the burly man I had spotted earlier, who had come lumbering along from the distant shadows. He was indeed a big fellow but my earlier fear soon evaporated as he greeted me warmly and broke into conversation. His name was Omine san, and apparently he knew the previous seller here and had been drinking with him a few times. His own job, as I had suspected, was with the local mob, which ran its own small version of 'soapland' or prostitutes' alley, in the building he had been lurking around. He had a look at my selection of rugby shirts and pointed to an extra-large one, saying he would buy it if I still had it after his pay-day. Seeing a large group of approaching males he loped off back to his base promising to pop back later.

I was relieved to make some sales, and enjoyed a few laughs with the locals, who were indeed very friendly. One solid, middle-aged man with dark glasses however, demanded roughly whether I had paid for my place as soon as he stepped out of his long black car, but I merely laughed it off with a deceptive nod, hoping I wouldn't live to regret it. Later, this worry was laid to rest by an affable youngster in a suit who was running around to check on all of the building's bars, as well as managing the karaoke box upstairs. He told me in fairly decent English that his father was the building's owner having had it built several years previously during Japan's property boom, and that he had been looking after it for him ever since. In common with nearly every other water business entrepreneur I had spoken to, his voice was full of gloom and doom on the subject of its future prosperity. Anyway, he was bored of it and couldn't wait to get back to America, he told me.

I had frequently heard from Budo about how the lowly seller in Japan can often attract those less conventional types in Japanese society who just don't quite fit in, otherwise known as *kawari-mono*. One such example had, only the previous day, spontaneously rushed up to embrace and kiss me before introducing himself as Tom. Apparently, he had only been abroad once, to London the previous year, though unfortunately all of his possessions had been stolen at Heathrow Airport. Despite this nasty experience, he was determined to visit America and to chase the American dream – whatever that might mean. He proudly showed me all his tattoos, which expressed his yearning for total individuality.

Takeo's *kawari-mono* was not quite like young Tom, but he was definitely not your run-of-the-mill Japanese male either. His name was Mori san and he was a science student at Fukuoka's Industrial University. He shocked me by purchasing my most expensive ring at Y5,000 without even trying to haggle over the price. He followed this up by bringing a four-pack of best lager for me ten minutes later, and then contentedly sat by my stall for the next three hours until closing time. Thinking he was just another one of life's lonely souls, I drank and chatted with him quite happily, until he suggested I sleep with him in his house, using the immortal line,

'I'm not gay but...'

I gently declined, as fortunately I had a genuine excuse in that I was moving straight on to Karatsu City after work. Evidently not one to take a hint easily, young Mori then put forward the idea that he could come too. I told him this was not a good idea, and awkwardly busied myself in serving three hostess customers.

When closing time came, Mori san persisted in making known his desire to come with me and was not in the slightest bit put off when I revealed that I would be sleeping in the van; in fact, he visibly warmed to the idea. Needless to say, I packed up my boards in double-quick time and was off like a bat out of hell, leaving the black leather-clad Mori standing forlornly in my wake. I immediately recalled the boast of an Ariake Town public servant back in 1989 and couldn't help scoffing out loud, 'So much for Japan's gayless society!'

12th March

Karatsu, with its population of eighty thousand, seemed like a metropolis after the decidedly rural city of Takeo. It listed an imposing traditional castle among its attractions, and seeing at least one other foreigner during my pre-lunch reconnaissance mission made me feel slightly more anonymous.

It did not take me long to locate the nightlife area, which basically constituted a narrow street by the river crammed full of *snakus*. Typically of such districts at this early hour, it was deserted, except for a burly young lad going about his beer deliveries. All the activity was in the arcade, just around the corner, where the locals were indulging in the much cited favourite Japanese pastime of window-shopping. I found a cheap and cheerful coffee shop where I ordered myself a *hi-gawari-teishoku* and settled down to my notes.

An hour later, I set about finding a *sentou*. Working on the premise that it was always quicker to ask, I approached an elderly gentleman, who had just come out of his house. He indicated that there was one nearby but that it would be simpler to show me on a map. He hurriedly re-entered his house only to reappear a few moments later beckoning me inside. I followed hesitantly.

What I had assumed to be his house turned out to be in fact an office on the ground floor, typified by an L-shape of grey desks with light green plastic covered tops. Three Japanese women in office uniform were frantically poring over three different local maps trying to decide on the exact position of this *sentou*, observing that it might well prove faster if the elderly gentleman – evidently the boss – took me there himself. Already totally embarrassed that my innocent question had brought a whole office to a standstill, I insisted that they ought not to go to any more trouble and that being pointed in roughly the right direction would suffice.

After further lengthy deliberation, the four of them finally reached a consensus of opinion as to the route I should follow, with various vending machines and barbers' shops as landmarks. I apologised for having interrupted their work and exited with a somewhat coy, 'Shitsurei shimashita,' in the appointed direction of 'Ebisuyu' bath-house, marvelling not for the first time at the obliging nature of the Japanese.

It did indeed turn out to be just around the corner. On arrival, I could hear the distinct sounds of hosing down from inside the locked door, and on being informed that it opened at four o'clock, I plumped for a short nap in the van, which I had parked in one of the two adjacent weed-ridden spaces.

At ten minutes to four, I paid my Y280 to the old woman at the desk, removed my shoes and stepped up into the men's changing room to the left of her. It was a tiny place with a makeshift partition separating it from the female section on the right. I was the first customer and revelled in having the place to myself. After putting my clothes in the locker, I pulled back the glass door leading into the bath and went in, shutting out the world behind me, though semi-conscious that the old woman was surveying the scene from time to time.

I continued to enjoy my solitude as I hand-washed my socks, pants and T-shirt. I then scrubbed myself clean with soap and rinsed my body before jumping into what was essentially no more than a two-man bath. Hot water was gushing from a lion-head tap, and steam rose up to the rough glass windows, through which sunlight was pouring directly on to my face. I closed my eyes and felt my body relax completely as I became lost in a serene paradise of my own. All of a sudden, the door was wrenched open, then pulled to with a mighty crack, sending echoes all around the room. This marked the entrance of an *o-jii-san* (old man) who, like a lot of older Japanese men, I had discovered, dispensed with the polite custom of washing off the day's grime at the nearby taps, instead plunging straight into my bath after whipping his long johns off.

Whether the old bugger suffered from a throat disorder of some description, I could not be sure, but from his tonsils emanated a permanent rasping growl resembling a broken-down traction engine, which was indeed somewhat disquieting at a distance of no more than two feet from my ear. In fact, the previous tranquillity and total naturalness of the bathing experience were shattered. This, coupled with the idea of someone else's body scum floating around my chin, spurred me to curtail the day's session by heading swiftly for the changing room.

★

Karatsu by night seemed to be quite lively. As I drove the van up to what I had earlier pin-pointed as the heart of the city's water-business, I felt slightly ill at ease because I could see three sleazy-looking men in black leather coats touting for business. They were, like Omine san in Takeo, obviously the lower orders of the *yakuza*, the types you find in most Japanese cities at night around the drinking-cum-prostitution districts. They have the unenviably seedy task of patrolling the streets for potential clients with the universal approach line, 'Dou desu ka?' ('How about it?')

I parked the van and made my way over to the youngest of the three and asked politely where the previous accessory sellers had set up shop. He indicated the front of a tall modern building to our right which had a paved area at one side of its entrance, facing directly onto the main drinking street. I thanked him, unloaded my stall, and drove off to a pre-selected spot about a kilometre away further down the river, where I hoped to park without a fine. I jogged back to the *saka-riba* with the usual apprehensive feeling that my goods might have been plundered, or that an irate shopkeeper might be lurking to complain about my presence. However, all was well – actually nobody was paying either me or my stall a blind bit of notice. As I set up, the young man stood over me and tried to assert an authority that he could doubtless only yearn for among his own order, by telling me to move my tables a couple of centimetres this way or that. Five minutes later, I was ready for business, although I really did feel like a genuine sleazeball standing at such close proximity to these whorehouse pimps. Nonetheless, despite my secret snobbery, I could certainly identify with them to a large extent, since they were invariably shrugged off like a bad smell! by the majority of their targeted prey – similar to the treatment I sometimes received when the more narrow-minded Japanese would stop specially to point out that I was a con-merchant.

The night was cold and business was slow. Despite a steady flow of passing traffic, few spared me even a second glance, let alone any serious intention to buy. I did not let this bother me, and continued to greet people with a gusty 'Konbanwa' or 'Irashaimase', moving around as I did so in an effort to keep warm. During the long five hours I spent there, I had ample opportunity to chat with two of the three *yakuza*. The young man, who had longish, greasy hair, apparently drove here each night all the way from Ureshino – a full one hour drive each way. He considered this to be a safe distance away from anyone who might recognise him. It seemed that I was not the only one concerned about being stigmatised. He revealed that he had a wife and three kids to support. His face told the whole story. Times were hard in this business, due to Japan's economic recession combined with a growing awareness of Aids, neither of which was commonly felt to apply to this country five years previously. He moaned that his commission-based salary was hardly enough to get by on – probably barely enough to finance his chain-smoking, I thought to myself. In spite of all this, he kindly bought me a can of hot coffee to 'combat the cold', as he put it.

Later on, I spoke with a second of the pimps. He was a squat, middle-aged man, who came across as being both nervous and extremely amiable. I learnt that he had been in the job for seven years, and that he thought it was high time he got promoted in the organisation. This seemed to me an unlikely prospect in a system based largely upon connections and ruthlessness. Nice, friendly members tended not to rise in the ranks. I tried to imagine myself spending three-quarters of a decade chasing drunks up and down the same street in all winds and weathers, and trying to ingratiate myself with them, only to be repeatedly treated like a piece of excrement. I supposed that the experience might lead to the thickening of one's skin if nothing else.

That same night, I met a rotund young man named Jun. He was a jovial character and, apparently, a friend of my predecessor. All of a sudden, he offered me a doctored telephone card – basically a used one with an illegally added metal strip on the back making it reusable. I had heard that these fake cards were produced solely by a group of Iranians in Osaka, and that one could obtain them only after the highest recommendation due to a recent high profile investigation forcing the fraudsters underground. I knew that most foreign street-sellers and the *yakuza* had access to these cards at roughly ten per cent of the price of the genuine article, but I was mildly shocked to find out that ordinary Japanese were also dealing in them. This made me wonder whether British Telecom was the victim of a similar scam in Britain. Anyway, I feigned ignorance of such cards but humoured his offer of a stack at a later stage should I give him the nod.

Up until midnight, I had sold virtually nothing, but a pair of love-hotel bound salarymen with their young *mizu-shoubai* mistresses helped to save my evening. What dream clients, I thought, as the girls pretended to hide their greed but went automatically for the most expensive necklaces, while their eager-to-please men-folk correctly cried, 'Nisemono da!' ('It's a damn fake!'), but coughed up the cash all the same. Who was it who said that Asian men carry their willies in their wallets? Probably a street-seller somewhere,

I chuckled, as I packed up my things and sped off back in the direction of Omura City.

20th March

Since this was my first night of business in Omura since my encounter with the immigration man and subsequent removal by the police, I was nervous when I set up shortly before eight o'clock. It being mid-week, Brick Street was very quiet. I tried to make myself as inconspicuous as possible by sitting hunched up on my low folding chair between the lamppost and my boards. Although I had intended to immerse myself in a Japanese book of idioms, my mind refused to focus and I looked warily at every passing car – a true case of paranoia.

I was relieved when I started to get some customers, because at least their conversations diverted my attention from its former preoccupation, and made me feel a little less like a spare part. A dapper middle-aged male in his forties fascinated me for the simple reason that his young female companion tonight was not the wife whom he had brought to my stall with their children in Isahaya the week before. I was still staring after them when a youth in a leather jacket piped up:

'That's a classic example of Japanese *furin*, you know.'

'What makes you say that?' I asked, realising that he was referring to a secret love affair, or to put it more technically, adultery.

'In my line of work, I see it every day, therefore, I can always recognise the telltale signs. You see, I work on reception at the plushest hotel in Omura. It is very common for wealthy Japanese businessmen or doctors to pay to have a room reserved all year just for that purpose. It is far more discreet than using a love hotel.'

'An exceedingly convenient arrangement, but a bit expensive for me,' I remarked.

'Have you got "furin" in your country?' he asked curiously.

'We used to have a lot of it,' I answered, my mind immediately homing in on the likes of Henry VIII. 'It must still exist now, though I don't imagine that many English women would take it lying down like yours seem to.'

'No, you're right there,' he acknowledged. 'Which makes you wonder whose women are actually stronger, doesn't it?'

This certainly gave me something to ponder for the rest of the night, as did the comment of one of my last customers, who apparently bought two London key-rings because he had so much enjoyed our long conversation:

'Of course, normally Japanese wouldn't dream of buying rubbish like this. However, you've kept me entertained in my own language for the last twenty minutes, so I think it's the least I can do.'

I had to smile at his honesty.

25th March

The last quarter of March marked the start of a fortnight's spring vacation for the schools. According to Budo, this was generally a time when Japan's street-sellers worked around the clock to make the most of all the wealthy but bored passing traffic. The other busiest, most profitable selling periods were Golden Week at the end of April; the summer vacation throughout August; and from the beginning of December right through to the middle of January because of Japan's great tradition of *Bounenkai* and *Shinnenkai* (Year End and New Year parties).

Naturally, on weekdays, I would not be able to occupy my usual weekend spot in front of Number 18 Bank, due to the bank being open for business, so I had made a note each day of which of the arcade's stores were closed for a day off. There was invariably a couple of options every day. I had also noticed that a large shoe shop at the main entrance to the arcade had been shut up ever since my arrival, obviously in preparation for some kind of renovation or refurbishment, so this provided even more scope. It was here that I set up that Monday.

As soon as I opened, a gang of young thirteen-year-olds came by and started trying on all the rings. I recognised the boys from my weekend sessions there – in fact, they had come the previous day and the Saturday before that. They seemed to be representative of their generation in that they were always well-clothed in the latest fashions, and when they passed my shop, they were always clutching bags containing their latest self-indulgences. Initially, I was surprised that so many of these youngsters could afford to buy my Y3,000 (£18) silver rings, but they did so without blinking an eyelid, sometimes on consecutive days. More often than not, they would open their wallets to reveal wads of notes worth more than a hundred pounds, and that was just for a local shopping trip. Even as an adult in my late twenties, I rarely carried that sort of money in my own country, and surely nobody could argue that the cost of living in London was any lower than in the rural regions of Kyushu.

Such signs of affluence reminded me of a conversation I had had some days before in the small Isahaya bath-house with an exceedingly humble and well-mannered dustman. He had voiced a belief common among those of his generation of post-war babies, that Japan's current decadence was the gateway to a long and slippery slope. He and his kind had been brought up in a poor country that had had to pick itself up and rebuild through hard work and determined spirit – qualities that the modern youth, born into the prosperity that followed, lacked completely. Today's children focused entirely on easy money and perpetual holidays – they were out of touch with reality because of having had everything handed to them on a plate. This attitude, he speculated, might well lead to Japan's next downfall. I could not help agreeing with him.

One of the young lads jerked me out of my reverie to pay for an earring, my best seller to date among young males. The group filed off, too hastily for my liking. Five minutes later I discovered that one of my rings was definitely missing. In spite of all this conspicuous affluence, the little rascals were happy to pilfer my accessories from right under my nose. Ten pence ring or gold bar, a thief is still a thief!

★

A biting cold wind, not to mention a scarcity of customers, had led me to close up in the middle of the afternoon and head for the small bath-house, which from my new position at the shoe shop, was just across the road.

The little old woman was there as usual at her counter separating the male from the female section. She was always ready for a good gossip.

'Now, where is it you said you came from?'
'London.'
'Yes, that's right. Italy, wasn't it?'
'Um, somewhere near there. England, actually.'
'Oh, my goodness...!' she cried, taking three steps backwards and looking visibly shaken. 'That's where they've got that cow disease, you know.'
'Yes, I had heard. Mind you, I've been eating beef twice a week for nearly thirty years and I'm still here.'

'You should change your diet to raw fish like the Japanese,' she advised gravely.

'Yes, perhaps I should,' I replied, heading for the bath, unable to imagine anything which would go worse with a pint of bitter.

27th March

A curious individual by the name of Shida san falteringly made his way to my shop on the morning of the 27th. A simple drunk, I thought at first, but a few moments of conversation told me that a reappraisal was in order; drunk he was, but simple he was not. It transpired that he was the master of a sushi restaurant out in the sticks somewhere to the west of Isahaya and that this was his one day off in a month. Apparently it was his custom every month on this day to venture into the relatively big city of Isahaya with Y100,000 (then roughly equivalent to £600) to blow it all on pachinko, beer and women.

We discussed a number of topics and it emerged that Mr Shida was a well-travelled person with a fair few experiences under his belt. He had worked hard to learn his trade in Osaka, but whether it was in this cosmopolitan centre or abroad that he had romanced the American woman whom he described in such uncomplimentary detail, I could not decide. Modesty forbids me to report his exact words as they are far from romantic, but he did liken part of the unfortunate female's anatomy to a bucket and bemoaned his inability as a Japanese to satisfy her. On the basis of this quick fling, Shida san had drawn the conclusion that all western women were built the same, therefore the men must be too. Sensing that he was looking to me for some kind of confirmation, I fell back on my stock response for this subject, which was that as far as I knew, there wasn't much to choose between the races.

He went on to condemn the paedophiliac element in his country, who indulge in the purchase of young girls' soiled underwear. By all accounts, this repulsive activity is rife, particularly in the larger cities, as is the practice of adults paying high school girls for dating and sex. Shida san protested that the perverts who fuel such booming businesses should have their testicles severed and served up as sushi, a fate that, in his view, should equally be applied to the countless secret child molesters in Japan.

After voicing his opinion on a few more domestic issues, Mr Shida bought three rings to be given later as presents to his favourite snack bar hostesses. Then he made off for the cinema, only to return a short time later as I was chatting to some junior high school girls. He jested around with them good-humouredly for a few moments before buying each of them a ring of their choice. They literally squealed with delight, and Shida san told me after they had gone that their pleasure was his pleasure.

Apparently the cinema was closed for some reason or other. Shida san urged me to shut up my shop and to join him for a few drinks. Despite the temptation, I resisted as I wanted to take advantage of the school holidays, which was why I had opened in the daytime, anyway. That I had already achieved my target thanks to Mr Shida's benevolence was beside the point. To work until five o'clock had been the plan, so work until five I would.

Not a man to be easily put off, he insisted that he would wait for me at a nearby raw fish *izakaya*. My scepticism that he would even remember, let alone still be upright at the appointed hour, proved unwarranted. He was sitting at the counter talking drunkenly to the master, a man in his sixties, who was apparently an old school friend. He seemed well-used to Shida san and his monthly binges.

Between five o'clock and seven o'clock, I enjoyed my first *izakaya* trip that March. I was treated to endless seafood delicacies with equal proportions of Kirin beer, even though by this stage – some fifteen pints into his own personal marathon – Mr Shida had degenerated into a burbling wretch and was knocking over everything in sight. I made my excuses just after seven, thanked my host very much, and left.

During the preceding two hours, I had downed my fair share of alcohol at ten times my normal rate, and it was just beginning to take its toll. I decided to return to the van for a brief snooze before the night shift. I went out like a candle only to wake up with a start and a thick head some three and a half hours later at after ten thirty. I forced myself to get behind the wheel and cursed my way to the night-life building that was no more than half a kilometre along the road. As I drew up, to my surprise, I found a crowd of female customers surrounding another foreigner who was doing business in my place – an impostor!

Unsure quite how to tackle the new situation, I pulled away to do another circuit in order to give myself time to think. According to Budo's rule book of street-selling:

'It's like a jungle out there, in this business. If somebody comes to your place, you must close him down immediately, without violence if possible. Should he resist, then you f—k him to the grave.'

I knew the theory as I had heard it all so many times before. However, I was not Budo; I did not consider that I, as a foreigner, owned any place in Japan, particularly on the street. Furthermore, the idea of being involved in yet another scrape was not very appealing.

By the time I pulled up for a second time, most of the customers had gone. Provoking a scene with a large audience had been a further reason for my hesitance, but with that excuse removed, I decided to take the bull by the horns. Jumping down from the van, I walked directly up to the seller. My sleepy grumpiness, coupled with my indignation, produced a very hostile mood indeed. I demanded to know what he thought he was doing, coming and setting up in the place I had been working for nearly six weeks now. Naturally, he pleaded ignorance of this fact, saying that he had been sent by someone else. Then, with a boyish grin he introduced himself as Aaron from Israel, and my English manners compelled me to shake his outstretched hand, even though I sensed that he was working for Zak, Budo's ex-partner and my ex-friend. I immediately confirmed this point, and although Aaron professed also to be a friend of Budo, I knew he was lying. The former partners' battle had now come to Nagasaki, and threatened to envelop me in a big way.

He remarked upon my hostility as I issued him with five minutes to shut his shop. He was able to make a hurried call to Zak, who apparently had a mobile phone, but I could not do the same because Budo, who would now be out selling, did not possess one. I noted that it was way past eleven o'clock. My enthusiasm for anything other than sleep was fast waning, and I was starting to think that it would be a waste of time setting up at this late stage anyway.

Aaron finished his phone conversation and suggested politely that we could compromise; he would stay open tonight and then move on the next day to a different place. This, coupled with the news that Zak and his friends were supposedly in neighbouring Omura, persuaded me to be reasonable and allow him the rest of the night. After all, I had arrived late and I didn't really fancy being heavily outnumbered in a battle which would inevitably result in my stall being smashed up and my jewellery stolen. I made my way back to the van trying to convince myself that my decision was an act of gentlemanly common sense, although I suspected that it would be seen by others to be more like a cowardly climb-down. I drove off towards Omura, ruing the beer and my resultant tardiness.

★

The next evening, I made an unprecedented move to get to Isahaya's Dai San Royal night-life building a full hour earlier than usual in order to claim my place and reverse the balance of power from what it had been the previous evening. It had been a sleepless night in the van because Budo's paranoia about Zak trying to score points over him here in Nagasaki had inflamed my own paranoia. I was afraid that I might be sabotaged or attacked in the dark by a band of fanatical Israelis. It was with this thought in my mind that I had finally lain down at five o'clock in the morning, after a heated telephone conversation with Budo, feeling more than a little agitated, despite a wrench and a baseball bat under my pillow for company.

The building was apparently empty, so I went about setting up my stall with Budo's stinging criticism still ringing in my ears,

'You have a big advantage when another seller comes to your place. He feels scared in the unfamiliar territory, whereas you should feel confident on your own ground. Your letting Aaron work tonight is, in this business, a sign of weakness – you and your f—ing English manners! He will be back and you must deal with him, no matter what it takes.'

The problem was that I did not consider it to be my own ground. But it wasn't his either, and it was a matter of pride. I resolved to do what I had to do so as not to lose face and so as not to present 'The Grape' with further ammunition with which to chastise me.

Budo's words were indeed quite prophetic. Aaron turned up a little after eight o'clock. I was relieved to see that he was alone. Apparently Budo had also been correct in identifying Aaron's claim that Zak was in Omura as a lie. It was part of his well-renowned psychological warfare – and thank the Lord for that, as I certainly did not fancy being attacked by a gang in a confined space that I could not possibly hope to escape from.

Aaron approached me without any particular menace in his eyes, although I could see that he was annoyed. He started to try and bargain with me, using the ploy of mutual identification.

'We are just the workers wanting to make quick money. Let's make a deal behind Zak and Budo's back.'

'Wrong,' I retorted. 'You are just a worker on your thirty-five or forty per cent. I, on the other hand, work with Budo and not for him, so I suggest you go and make your deals elsewhere. You know the Israeli street-selling territory rule as well as I do.'

Aaron attempted to persuade me for another ten minutes that it would be in my interests to reach a compromise, though the thinly-veiled menace in his voice merely strengthened my stance. Resigned to my intransigence, he disappeared into the night, vehemently threatening me with imminent death at the hands of Zak and his ruthless friends.

5th April

The day was glorious and Omura Park was as full of cherry blossom as it was of *O-hanami* (flower viewing) merrymakers. After a reasonable day's business in Isahaya, I had stopped off at the park for a beer and a nap. Finding a place to leave the van was only marginally more difficult than securing an empty patch of grass, as large blue tarpaulin sheets lay end to end marking the reservation of space for company parties. Those not already jam-packed with sake-swilling businessmen were guarded by office lady sentries or other company underlings frantically laying on a spread for their senior colleagues, who would arrive later, to devour it. Today was a Friday, which only heightened the buzz of excitement in the air. I contemplated setting out my stall but decided to settle for the nap in the end, thinking I would surely sell well later on amidst such feverish excitement.

Two hours later, at my usual spot in Brick Street, I discovered the error of my thinking. True, at eight o'clock, the usually quiet *saka-riba* streets were swarming with mixed groups of flower viewers seeking to prolong the annual event with a session or two of karaoke, but today's imbibers seemed somehow disinterested in imported accessories. In fact, they were obnoxious and penny-pinching. Two punches in the chest from a xenophobic drunken construction worker, and a mountain of verbal abuse set the tone for the night to come. Not wishing to scupper future selling in this area, I responded to none of it, although I did fantasise about meeting the waist-high builder under a different set of circumstances and engineering his excruciatingly gruesome demise.

The police were running around, seemingly dealing with all sorts of intemperate behaviour. Fortunately they were too busy to pay me even scant attention, though my stomach churned whenever their two-tone cars were in the vicinity. At such times, I would either shrink behind my stall or indulge in animated conversation with any browsing customers which was how I got talking to a Tokyo novelist who stopped by at about half past nine.

He was an omniscient little fellow, instantly following his self-introduction with a lecture on London geography and the origins of various British names. There is nothing guaranteed to irk an Englishman more than having to tolerate a foreigner attempting to educate him about his own country, especially if that foreigner is indeed better informed on the subject than he is himself. I listened as patiently as possible, concluding that here was yet another harmless, lonely soul, whose incredibly boring torrent of useless information had probably sent any potential spouse running for cover, just as a pair of female customers did when he opportunistically invited them to join him for a drink.

Resigned to a night of his own company, he resorted to testing me on more linguistic definitions, pausing at regular intervals to blow his own trumpet, so to speak, with the words, 'I bet you've never met anyone as interesting as me.'

There was no answer to that.

Nevertheless, revenge was sweet when I managed to floor him an hour or so later with an archaic Japanese proverb regarding a bat in a birdless village. I got a perverted pleasure from watching the man who had been a mine of foreign information baffled by the significance of one of his own country's expressions – not that I expected otherwise having failed to get a satisfactory answer from at least a score of local folk spanning three generations. Soon after this he left, racking his brains and swearing to return when he had researched the answer. I did not tell him that I too had not the faintest idea what the answer was, because he didn't ask.

7th April

Five o'clock that Sunday evening, signalled the end of a busy weekend and the start of my only night off. Intent on a slightly more luxurious bath than the preceding six days of the week, I parked my van under Isahaya's Green Hotel and trudged up the stairs to its sauna bath-house.

It was sheer bliss as I lay back in the spacious hot bathtub and reflected first upon my day, and then upon my life in general. The naked bronze figurine above me seemed almost poised to share in my idle contemplation, and perhaps to give me in turn the benefit of her sacred pearls of wisdom. At this stage, I was joined in the water by a bespectacled gentleman named Kurota san. I vaguely recalled his face from a previous meeting, which soon made sense when he held out a right hand displaying one of my imitation rings. He was obviously a regular bather here, because, come to think of it, I had seen him on my previous visit. We talked for a few minutes before he asked me if I would like to go with him for a few drinks at his favourite *snaku* later on. He struck me as a pleasant man and, unlike those of so many people, his opening questions – so far – had not been at all intrusive, so I happily accepted.

It was still only just after six o'clock. I ordered a few bottles of Kirin beer and poured for Kurota san as we lay back in our pyjamas upon the reclining chairs to watch television in the men's lounge. I started to feel rather mellow, and might have considered the experience all the more ideal, had there not been a cloud of smoke billowing out from just about every mouth in the room. I could never figure out why it was that the Japanese had to smoke so much, especially after having gone to the trouble of cleansing their bodies in a steaming hot bath.

At seven o'clock, we made our way back to the changing room to slip into our fresh clothes. I stopped for a moment to watch the blind masseur at work in the adjoining salon, and could not help marvelling at his amazing dexterity, for he had already kneaded and pummelled his client to sleep. I paid for the beers and we left and began walking up the now deserted arcade towards the river. On entering his *snaku*, Kurota san was greeted like a visiting celebrity. The Mama san and her customers were all of a similar vintage (forty-something) which went towards explaining the warm reception, for the place was apparently run and frequented by his schoolmates.

For the rest of the night, we indulged in endless karaoke, laughter, whisky, and all manner of gastronomic delights. A school friend of Mr Kurota and the Mama san, called Junko, sat next to me at the counter most of the night. She was an inquisitive woman – to put it mildly – continually demanding to know what my job was and how we had met. However, my new-found drinking partner discreetly avoided her questions, whilst I was equally evasive, too ashamed to admit to the lowliness of my current profession. She, on the other hand, was not blessed with the same tactful qualities, and made it plain that she was partial to a bit of male *gai-jin* by snuggling ever closer as her inebriation increased. Had I been five times as stoned – and had she been less like a horse – I might have been tempted to act out our singing duets, but I think these alone were dire enough for the others to endure.

It was a good night, though, at the end of it, I was none the wiser as to the occupation of Kurota san. Junko, however, was soon to discover my deep dark secret, since she passed my shop some days later. She scowled, put her head down as low as it would go and carried on walking.

12th April

In anticipation of a fruitful Friday night, I opened promptly at eight o'clock. An hour later, I was doing brisk business when Aaron's van pulled up. He drove straight at my trestles and swerved at the last moment just brushing the stall with his bumper. He got out and took up a position behind my shop after we had exchanged forced pleasantries.

I continued serving a young hostess from one of the nearby *snaku* bars when Aaron started offering pierced earrings to her friend. I rather too sharply pointed out in Japanese that he was nothing to do with my business and that I would serve her in a moment. The confused hostess, who could not possibly believe that not all foreigners were friends, shot me a strange look and then, as if sensing trouble, she hastily departed along with her girlfriend and all the other customers.

Aaron started to spin a hard-luck tale about how he had just driven all the way from Saga City, having been forced to pay most of his week's profits to the *yakuza*. He complained that because he was at the end of his strength, he could not possibly drive any further, and that therefore he intended to open up his *basta* right next to mine. One look at his eyes was enough for me to realise that he was in a tired and desperate mood. I knew that I had trouble on my hands. Without a doubt, he had seen my actions at our previous confrontation as a sign of weakness and assumed that he could now walk all over me whenever he felt like it.

'I obviously made a mistake with you the first time we met in thinking that you would be decent enough to move on and find your own place. I should have closed you there and then,' I said hotly.

'Oh, so you made a mistake, did you? I'm going to open right now,' he said threateningly.

'Fine. Do so and I will be forced to close you. Why don't you use your brain? If your objective really is to make money, open up elsewhere. There is simply not room for two of us here.' By 'elsewhere', I meant Ureshino, but I had no intention of spelling it out for him.

He suddenly darted over to his van, pulled out his trestles and started setting up less than four metres away from my shop. Instinctively, I went up to him and immediately took them apart. He quickly turned on me, raising one of the three-foot-long plywood boards in both hands above his head. I backed away slowly, keeping my eyes on the raised board.

'So let's fight!' he shouted, dropping the board and striding back to the corner to take his lumberjacket off. Resigned to the fact that the time for diplomacy had passed, I raced to do likewise, determined not to show fear. I couldn't help reckoning my chances to be no better than evens – I was taller and trained regularly for football; he was more compact and looked as though he wasn't long out of the Israeli army – a chilling prospect!

The first to disrobe, I went straight towards him. He automatically picked up the trestle again and raised it above his head as before. I assumed a pseudo karate-style stance and thinking that attack might well be the best form of defence, moved directly into the path of the descending board that Aaron made to bring crashing down upon my head. With my flexed left arm raised to block the wooden weapon, I planned a quick shimmy and a hard right in the face so as to get at least one good punch in before ultimately being beaten.

To my enormous surprise, he aborted at the last possible moment, and backed off releasing the board with the words, 'You're good.'

He set about putting his things back in his van and drove off. I watched him go, conscious that Brick Street was uncharacteristically quiet for a Friday night. I was also aware that my legs were now shaking violently and that my heart was pounding in harmony. I considered myself fortunate not to be wearing a trestle on my head and thanked God for having given me the strength to call Aaron's bluff.

That night, I went on to make Y61,000 (£380). It was my most lucrative night to date.

13th April

I finished my day-shift in the arcade about £150 better off and then went to freshen up in Isahaya Park's public conveniences before driving on to Takeo for the evening stint. On the ledge, where I usually put my wash bag, lay an abandoned plastic bag. Natural curiosity led me to prod it and when I realised there was something inside, I could not resist taking a quick peek. After all, about a fortnight previously a similar find at the same location had resulted in five minutes of private perving as the deserted carrier bag I had stumbled on contained a pile of exceedingly graphic 'men only' magazines. No depraved titillation this time, however, as the bag revealed a leather wallet containing Y40,000 in cash (over £250), a list of telephone numbers, and a bundle of credit cards bearing the *kanji* (Chinese character) name *Nishikawa*.

There was nobody in the cubicles. I hesitantly picked up the bag and searched around outside for a possible owner, to no avail. I cursed my luck because the last place I wanted to go to announce my presence was the local police station, but I really had no alternative. I could imagine the owner going frantic over his loss just as I had done twice in the space of a month two years previously in Kumamoto City having carelessly lost two wallets that both failed to reappear.

I slowly made my way to the police box, which I knew was just around the corner, preparing to field any awkward questions should they arise. It was a modern, circular building, its front entrance made up of two huge automatic glass sliding doors leading into an unexpectedly poky reception area with three dull grey desks placed side by side in a line. Behind these were seated two male uniformed officers on telephones and a female officer shuffling some papers. My arrival was greeted with three sets of raised eyebrows and a startled look on the face of the young female whose desk I approached, but she visibly relaxed when I greeted her and explained myself in Japanese.

My rather optimistic hope that I might be able simply to drop the wallet on her desk and run for the hills was dashed as the WPC produced a mountain of forms. Apparently one of these made provision for two-fifths of a retrieved wallet's cash to be rewarded to the finder, should the owner not come forward to claim it within a specified period of time. Still hoping to slip off with the minimum fuss, I insisted that there was no need for that, which only led to her insisting even more vehemently that it was the law. Consequently I went through the ritual of filling the forms in with the kind assistance of the policewoman, who helped speed the process up considerably.

Ten minutes later, we were just about finished when the senior policeman sitting to the right of her, having finished his telephone conversation, officiously butted in, barking out in English:

'Name? Address? Telephone?'

He continued in this vein for a full five minutes with his unnecessary English, despite the poor girl subtly trying to point out that we had already covered this ground in Japanese which I could seemingly speak quite adequately.

It was quarter to five before I climbed into my van and set off in the direction of Takeo, musing on the lengths some people will go to in order to try to assert their authority.

18th April

A group of young men burst into Isahaya's Dai San Royal Building shortly before eleven o'clock on the night of

Thursday, 18th April. Slightly ahead of the rest, the first, a scrawny gangling youth dressed in faded denim jeans and brown cowboy boots, snatched up my stool and launched it high into the air so that it came down with a crash at some distance from my *basta*. He appeared completely oblivious to my presence, and it took only a glance at his bleary red eyes to see that he was totally inebriated.

Up to this moment, I had been in a fairly mild mood after an early evening hot bath and two rugby shirt sales immediately on opening, but not mild enough to allow such uncalled for abuse of my possessions to pass unchallenged. I asked him to explain himself. He looked at me, but his wild, bloodshot eyes refused to focus and he merely replied with a slurred question of his own as to the whereabouts of a *snaku* called 'Sasou'. I calmly persisted with my question and demanded an apology. I was conscious that a sizeable group of eight or nine of his friends had by now joined him and was surrounding us. Their noisy entrance was replaced by an ominous silence, and I was half wishing that I had stayed in the bathtub.

All of a sudden two of his friends, who had obviously witnessed the proceedings, apologised profusely for him, one getting down on his knees and bowing at my feet. Then, a taller, more mature individual, with shoulder-length hair and wearing a leather waistcoat, with similar cowboy boots, made his way into the building, deep in conversation with another youth. As he approached, the group moved to let him pass. He was evidently their *senpai* or senior member. Taking the scene in at a glance, and with a few hurriedly whispered reports from his juniors, he took hold of the lanky young Cowboy Boots, smacking him twice in the face. After an apology was beaten out of the youth for his drunken craziness, I almost regretted having made a fuss.

They all trooped off to their appointed *snaku* bar, which turned out to be on the first floor, just above my head. However, right into the early hours of the morning, one after another of them returned to my shop to purchase rings or bracelets, continuing to apologise for the earlier incident, to the point where I was most embarrassed by their excessive humility. I tried to imagine myself in a similar situation with a group of drunken louts in Britain and swiftly concluded that I was glad it had happened in Japan.

23rd April

With the end of my pseudo-nomadic existence fast approaching, I opened my stall in a particularly good mood that night in Takeo. I marked the occasion by treating Omine san to a half-litre can of lager, and we stood for ten minutes, side by side, supping contentedly.

Apparently, he had already enticed a drunk old man into his soapland building – quite a coup so early in the evening. Purely as a matter of interest, I asked him how much it would cost for a session with one of his girls and he quoted the price of Y20,000. However, he assured me that I could have a special discount if I were interested. His offer came as some surprise, because I had heard that foreigners were not permitted in such places due to the Japanese fear of the so-called 'foreign disease' – Aids. Omine san said that this was not applicable to anyone who is given a personal introduction and recommendation by a member of the organisation, such as himself. He went on to explain that most foreigners are barred on the basis of their not being able to speak Japanese, and thus not understanding the strict rules of the establishment which could lead to trouble. He pointed out that since this also did not apply to me, there was no problem. His revelation certainly gave me food for thought.

Before business started to get brisker at ten o'clock, a smart gentleman in his early forties stopped by to cast a cursory glance over my wares. He had a stern face, and was evidently self-confident as he opened up with a string of personal questions that took the form of a mini-interrogation. I answered politely, but in a light-hearted manner, probably due to the beer. Before long, he too lightened up and told me all about his daughter, who was planning to do a homestay abroad to improve her English. He asked my advice, and I predictably blew my own metaphoric trumpet, extolling the virtues of good old Great Britain.

We continued to chat along these lines for at least ten minutes before he bought a silver ring for Y3,000. While handing over the money, he told me to call him if I encountered any problems on the street. After passing me his business card, he rushed off to his appointment, with the parting advice that I should move to a larger city if money was my chief goal. On looking at his card, I saw that he was a sub-boss in the Nagasaki Prefectural police.

As I slipped the card into my wallet, I realised that an old man was relieving himself against the wall at the end of my stall. I regarded him with distaste. Despite my disapproving looks, he staggered up to me after he was done and expressed a desire to shake my hand. More conscious than ever that the Japanese are more or less without exception right-handed in everything they do, I proffered my left hand so as not to appear unfriendly. I might as well not have bothered though, because he shook it with his right hand anyway.

At this point, Omine san popped up with a few choice words and ushered the eager old chap off on his way, leaving me to avoid the stream in the gutter of his fast-flowing urine.

The midnight hours saw the successful sale of my most expensive accessory item to date; an imitation gold necklace for Y10,000, or a mere £60. Even though the rich businessman correctly identified it as a fake, he could do nothing but yield to the voracious materialism of the stunning teenage hostess on his arm. From the look in her eyes, and his extreme magnanimity, I could tell that this was far from the final chapter in their story.

Just as another ageing individual was scanning my collection of erotic rings (those sculpted in the shape of naked bodies indulging in various positions of the sexual act), the door of a first floor *snaku* bar opposite burst open, and down the stone steps raced a ten-strong group of young males to do a quick sprint up the length of the street. Nothing unusual about that, you might think, except that they were totally naked.

They ran back a minute later, all of them clasping their tools, and disappeared back into the *snaku* bar, greeted by hysterical cackles from the applauding girls. My customer, meanwhile, had found two positions which took his fancy and passed over the money, advising me to arrange better lighting around my stall if I wanted my sales to improve in the future.

Having made a reasonable profit, I trundled along to Omine san and presented him with the only remaining extra-large rugby shirt, which he had previously admired. I had decided that it was about time for me to give something back to the Japanese people and besides, he was a nice fellow. Omine san was touched with emotion and promised that he would treasure it for the rest of his days.

Takeo's soapland was just about to close for the night, but I stayed open to try and catch any straggling drinkers. Ten minutes later, I watched Omine san pass with his van-load of girls. He gave a big wave as he rounded the corner, leaving me to wonder exactly what their motivation was for doing a job like that, and asking myself whether I was any different.

26th April

The Friday before Golden Week arrived, heralding the final ten day countdown to my return to Kumamoto and civilisation as I knew it. The warmer weather had also finally come, not to mention the azalea in Omura park, which was pink and profuse under a totally cloudless blue sky. The muddied pond was a mass of gaping jaws as fish and wildfowl fought greedily over the breadcrumbs offered by a little girl. A snake slid silently by in the distance, gliding effortlessly on the surface of the water towards a tiny, wooded island, and then disappeared from sight.

I was reading the previous Friday's Yomiuri newspaper seated on the grass overlooking the pond, when I became aware of a middle-aged man grinning over my shoulder. I bid him an affable 'Konnichiwa' and he nodded in greeting. He continued to hover there and it was a full three minutes before he dispelled my growing suspicions that he might be dumb by remarking, 'How nice it must be to be able to read English!'

'Well, yes, I suppose it is,' was my automatic response. 'Mind you, it would be far more useful over here to be able to read Japanese to a decent level.'

He did not acknowledge this point, but instead slipped briefly into the customary game of humility and flattery before launching into something entirely different with the statement, 'It's a good job we didn't win the war, you know. It's thanks to America defeating us and forcing us to start all over again on a new political and psychological footing that we have achieved what we have today. If we had won the war, we would simply have carried on in the old, intransigent *samurai* way and would not have developed into half the power we are now. We must be grateful to you Americans for this. I don't know much about American society, though, so perhaps you could enlighten me.'

'Well, never having been to the US I can't tell you much, I'm afraid. Actually, I'm from England,' I said, trying not to sound too proud.

'Aha, the country with the Royal Family in turmoil.'

'We do have our problems in that area, yes. However, you must take into account that everything is greatly magnified and exacerbated by a sensationalist media,' I retorted, unable to control my royalist tendencies.

'Yes, we are fortunate in Japan because strict laws forbid our press to write negative things about our Royal Family. Of course, being human, we too have many skeletons in the cupboard, but heavy censorship allows us to conceal these aspects and only the positive stories are printed.'

I was pleasantly astounded by such an honest confession. For years I had been battling to point out the very same thing in an attempt justly to counter Japanese glee at Prince Charles' troubles. I abhorred their hypocritical tendency to lap up all the tabloid gossip with total gullibility, and the way they delighted in elevating their own royals (apparently they do exist) at our expense. The well-worn Japanese expression 'complex' – as in inferiority – when viewing themselves in comparison to many things Caucasian, would have been far more apt here, I felt, than in the trifling everyday contexts for which it was so frequently used.

Having aired his opinions on royalty, Mr Nikko went on to cover Saddam Hussein, the Vietnam war, the American civil service and Chinese cultural history, before thanking me for the exchange of ideas and returning to work at the education section of the nearby town hall. I resumed reading my newspaper, remembering how lucky I was to be able to read English.

28th April

I decided to open in Omura, instead of taking my usual Sunday night off in Kuwa-Kuwa sauna and swilling my stomach with endless glasses of ale. The next day was a public holiday, the first day of Golden Week, so in theory there ought to be a lot of people out drinking tonight, provided that is they hadn't all jumped in their cars to head off for a real holiday.

For seven years, casual enquiries on the subject had invariably produced the same Japanese response:

'Plans for Golden Week? You must be joking! Japan's incredibly narrow roads are all packed with cars as tightly as sushi in a box – you can't move for traffic. No, we're going to stay at home this year and avoid the crowds.'

So where on earth did all those people in the widely televised nationwide fifty-mile tailbacks come from year in year out? Surely they couldn't all be foreigners.

As I had predicted, there was indeed a fair bit of activity down Renga-Doori and it wasn't long before I got off the mark by selling a couple of the smaller items. At an early stage, I was joined by a skinny, forty-something man whose name was Seiji. He was dressed in a shabby, ill-fitting suit, which looked as though it had just been slept in, and he reeked of alcohol, not to mention stale tobacco. Despite his insistence on smoking right under my nose, he was a harmless sort, I deduced, and evidently lonely into the bargain.

Seiji tottered from side to side as we spoke about this and that. During the course of our conversation, he insisted I find time to go to his apartment to enjoy the thrills offered by his one hundred strong collection of uncensored hard-porn videos. Apparently, he habitually left the place unlocked, so I could drop in any time I pleased. He issued this invitation almost as many times as he asked my name, which, had he been sober, he would have remembered by his predictable 'Luke over there' witticism. He finally went, but was back within ten minutes, having brought his pet hamster to show me. Had he not failed to recall my name yet again, he could have done the introductions himself. Budo (as the hamster was coincidentally called), was not amused at this sudden trip into the outside world. The poor little chap was shaking like a leaf and seemed far more content to cower under Seiji's jacket – obviously a braver fellow than me, I thought. Not being too keen on rodents of any description, I showed little or no interest in Budo, so the two soon departed, much to my relief, as I was growing tired of humouring Seiji and his smoke.

The street was reasonably quiet now. A tall, striking-looking girl in a black leather jacket and tight Levi's passed confidently in front of my shop. She warmly returned my greeting with a radiant smile. Refreshingly original, I mused, since the average solo female response seemed to be nervous laughter bordering on outright fear. She walked past my shop several more times in the next ten minutes, I noticed, as I was serving other customers, and on one of these occasions I piped up jokingly:

'You're doing a lot of walking tonight, aren't you?'

She grinned.

'Yes, I'm bored with nothing to do. I was going to my friend's shop but it's closed.'

She bent over my shop, and I couldn't help weighing her up from a male point of view after two months of my own company: decent sized breasts that almost fell out of a low cut tank top and half cup bra; long, shapely legs with a strong firm backside accentuated by the tight cut of the

Levi's; lightly permed, shortish hair, and a striking face – not beautiful by any means, but attractive in an animal-magnetic type way – with a large, rouged mouth and relatively big eyes. Her teeth were rather prominent, but all in all, I judged, everything went together jolly well.

I guessed that this girl had to be about twenty and was probably a student of some description, though a quick glance at the roughness of her hands made me wonder if she was training to be a carpenter. The anomaly was soon explained when she introduced herself as Yukie, telling me in the next breath that she worked in a petrol station, which was the reason for her hands being in the state they were.

We talked light-heartedly for some time before Seiji returned on a bright red scooter brandishing what looked suspiciously like the leftovers of his cat's dinner for me – kind thought; awful timing. He unreservedly joined our conversation, immediately pointing out the size of Yukie's breasts. She giggled coquettishly which, in turn, triggered some kind of reaction around my loins. In my mind, I was already bedding this lass, taking out all of my frustrations, living out every sexual fantasy... and then Seiji fell over my shop.

It took a little while to straighten my boards and display cases out again, and when I'd finished, Yukie bent over again to inspect my wares. Soon, quite a crowd had gathered, under the pretence of looking at my rings, but really they were gawping at Yukie's cleavage. Two young men even had the audacity to assume positions either side of me behind the shop where the view was substantially better, not that I had been looking, of course. Yukie feigned oblivion to the *skebe* (lascivious sods) but she would have had to have been blind and deaf as well as totally senseless not to realise what was going on.

After great deliberation, Yukie decided to buy a wallet and a ring for Y7,000, almost completely emptying her purse in the process. I was half reluctant to take so much money off her, so I gave her the small imitation ring, which she had also previously been toying with as a present, in an effort to appease my conscience.

Seiji again disappeared only to return five minutes later with two hamsters exploring the odours beneath his jacket. If he thought these cute little creatures were going to endear him to Yukie, he was very much mistaken, because she apparently found rodents as repulsive as I did and told him so in no uncertain terms. This pronouncement sent all three of them scurrying off with their tails between their legs.

By now, it was gone half past eleven and Brick Street was buzzing with life. Those who were just about to start on a session of hostess karaoke, were eager to get in somewhere to enjoy a decent spell before closing time, whereas those who had been on the *hashigo* all night were well past wanting to go home anyway. Yukie appeared in no hurry to go anywhere, as she hung around my stall while I attended to other customers. A car pulled up and a youth, whom I'd asked earlier in the evening about beer-vending machines, wound down the window and handed me a chilled half-litre can of Heineken. I felt awkward when he refused payment for it, and it was at this point that Seiji, who had since returned hamsterless, took it upon himself to give me a lecture about it being offensive in Japan to offer money to someone who is presenting you with a gift out of kindness. I resented the lecture, pointing out that although I was extremely familiar with Japanese generosity, it often did nothing to accommodate one's own sense of pride and principles, particularly in this case, as I had earlier raised the beer machine question myself purely because I wanted to save the Y200 slapped on a bottle at the nearby *raamen* shop. While I was at it, I took further pains to point out that surprising as it might sound, (by this I was in fact referring to my lowly position on the street) I was not in the habit of feeding off anybody like a parasite. Seiji's expression was a picture of utter bewilderment, and I am not sure he even registered that he had hit a raw nerve.

Yukie was still hanging around and continued to humour Seiji while I went about my business. He bought her a London key-ring and I overheard him saying that he wasn't interested in sex, just a healthy chat. I turned my head away, unable to resist guffawing into my left shoulder. He asked Yukie my name at least another three times and then disappeared again. She stayed a little longer, but unfortunately, I was with customers and unable to talk to her, therefore, after a few more minutes, she made off with a wave, a smile and the eternal, 'Mata ne!' ('See you around!') which was the last I saw of her.

The irrepressible Seiji reappeared once more, but I had run out of patience, so he did not stay long, nor did he return again. I was left with my unfulfilled erotic thoughts, and concluded that it was all for the best.

29th April

Between the day-shift and the night-shift, I felt the need to use the Isahaya Park public facilities. On entering one of the two cubicles, I stumbled upon an abandoned pair of boxer shorts with a large turd flattened to the inside – a fairly revolting discovery, which prompted me to switch to the neighbouring cubicle. However, I couldn't suppress a lingering smirk as I squatted there.

At regular intervals throughout the evening I had this recurring image of some poor fellow in a business meeting with bulging trousers trying to plead, 'Not guilty!' I sniggered every time, though whether it was out of some sort of feeling of superiority or merely out of pure human identification, I was not sure. Whichever, it had made a fairly potent impression upon me and probably anybody else who came across it.

An example of its powerful entertainment value manifested itself later on after my night-shift when I returned to sleep in the adjacent car park. I was just savouring the last few drops of a small can of Sapporo Black Label beer and, wallowing in the tranquillity of the early morning, when a young couple pulled up. They spent some time doing what young lovers do in the comfort of their vehicles, before getting out and going over to the lavatories. After a moment or so, I heard the young man call urgently over to the girl from the gents' side, and within a few seconds, they both came out again, splitting their sides, shrieking with raucous laughter,

'Gamin dekinakatta'n da' ('He couldn't quite make it').

This triggered my laughter mechanism – yet again – as I sucked on my empty beer tin with the thought that this fascinating spectacle could be included as a comic tourist attraction, since it was definitely far more effective than any laughing gas I had ever heard of, although I genuinely did feel for the owner of the boxers.

1st May

I set up rather furtively in Omura arcade at lunchtime, hoping to maximise my profits in this last week of Golden Week. I had always been wary of opening up here in broad daylight, not only because Omura boasted an exceedingly large and active immigration office, but also because I knew that a certain Englishman by the name of Mike had been given his marching orders for persisting to sell here a couple of years previously. I suppose the fact that the police had taken my name and moved me on shortly after my arrival in Nagasaki Prefecture had increased my paranoia.

Early that morning, I had carried out a reconnaissance mission to find the best place in which to open. It was a choice between the more spacious area directly in front of the Fuji Bank, and the more compact spot in front of a disused *pachinko* parlour. I plumped for the latter, concluding that its location at the heart of the arcade would result in a greater volume of passing shoppers whilst not exposing me to the main road and its patrolling police cars. Besides, nobody was likely to object to me blocking the entrance to this dilapidated former centre of noisy amusement.

I wasn't open long before an ageing suit from the MFI-style furniture shop opposite walked over to me rather purposefully and, dispensing with all introductory exchange of pleasantries, stuck an aerosol can right under my nose.

'Here, could you just translate these English instructions on this furniture spray for me? It's just arrived from abroad, and I can't read a word of it.'

I took the canister, and instantly recognised that what he had mistaken for English was in fact Spanish. If the truth were known, he had probably not consciously identified it as English. No doubt he had simply registered that it was foreign and had applied the well-used Japanese strain of logic that being foreign, I was therefore perfectly equipped to read it.

'These instructions are in Spanish,' I pointed out.

'Yeah, yeah, don't worry about that. Just tell me what it means in Japanese.'

'Well, I've never actually studied Spanish before. You see, I'm from Britain.'

'What language do you speak there, then?' he asked.

It was at this stage that I decided that it might be better all round if I had a stab at giving him some kind of rendering in Japanese. After all, I had majored in Italian and French at university, so at least I did have some sort of common root to draw upon, even if such knowledge had been lying dormant for almost seven years. I stumbled through it less than fluently, but in the end, he seemed satisfied with my rough translation. After querying one small point, the difference between 'dust' and 'dirt', he turned abruptly back to his shop with the comment, 'Don't know why these foreign companies can't print their instructions in Japanese instead of English.'

Shortly after this, Seiji walked meekly up, this time cradling a kitten in place of a hamster, but he did not stay for more than a minute, before walking off again, equally meekly.

6th May

Golden Week had finally come to an end. It had not been quite as profitable as I had been led to expect by Budo, but I had managed to sell all of my British sports shirts and was only left with a handful of Scottish Guardsmen magnets. The jewellery, too, had sold well.

On my way back to Kumamoto, I spent some time on the monotonous Kyushu Expressway, analysing the value of my recent outdoor experience. Without a doubt, from a financial point of view, it had been a triumph, for I had actually managed to save in just nine weeks more than I could usually put by in a year. On the other hand, expensive drinking slaloms had been off the agenda, so my earnings had been basically all for saving, since I did not have any domestic bills or rent to consider either.

Apart from the money, I had enjoyed the opportunity to meet countless people, with whom I had been able to practise my spoken Japanese daily for hours on end.

Therefore, linguistically, it had also been a success, not to mention satisfying for anyone like myself who is interested in languages. However, for the average foreign seller, who has to get by mainly in English, customer conversations in Japan would be exceedingly limited. Not having the chance for any really meaningful verbal exchanges over a long period of time could easily lead to frustration and loneliness, the symptoms of which were plain to see in both Budo and Mike (a Sasebo City seller).

In the short term, such a simple, free way of life is very attractive, allowing one the chance to step back and put things into perspective. Nevertheless, the street existence in Japan is a solitary one, as relationships with most of the Japanese are restricted to a superficial level, and so it does not give much scope for glimpses of the real culture and customs that I had been fortunate enough to witness when I was in the 'acceptable' profession of English teaching. In the long term, for me, no amount of riches would compensate for the lack of social integration, not to mention the consequent lack of self-esteem.

Arriving back in the familiar city of Kumamoto, I felt as if I had stepped back into my other, more real world. When I dropped the van off at Budo's and squared up with him, his wife handed over a present that had come in the post for me some days earlier. It was a beautiful dragon mosaic picture as an expression of thanks from a man called Nishikawa san, the owner of the wallet in Isahaya.

That night, I went out for a drink in the city with my Japanese footballing friends. In reply to their enquiries about what I had been doing for so long up in Nagasaki, I told them I had been travelling. They naturally assumed that I had been seeing a woman. I just smiled, thinking that nothing could have been further from the truth.

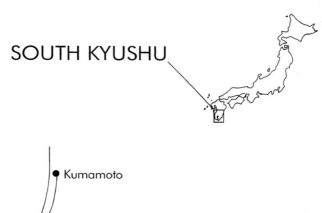

March 1997

I had returned to Japan at the end of February on an uncertain footing. Budo was keen for me to play a role in the *basta* business down in Kagoshima City but I was unwilling to be part of such a stigmatised trade in a place where I knew so many people. On the other hand, I was eager to do more research on the subject of street-selling, and I wanted to devote time to studying karate. With these two factors as my main priorities, re-entering the teaching world on an inflexible full-time Japanese contract was neither feasible, nor at that stage particularly appealing.

In early March, Budo and I went down to Kagoshima City by car where we met up with a young Japanese woman called Yumiko, who was said to be the contractual wife of Budo's good friend, Mishak. Mishak considered himself to 'own' this city in street-selling terms but was apparently back in Israel studying. Seemingly, he had agreed to rent it out for Y400,000 a month, and would arrange to send workers. Budo had promised to help him out, but running his own stall in Kumamoto City, which was two hundred kilometres away, made things rather difficult. Since I was planning to live in Kagoshima again for a while, I said that I would be prepared to lend a hand behind the scenes, providing I approved of the set-up. I made it clear that on no account would I sell on the streets.

Yumiko was perhaps the most unfeminine Asian woman I had ever come across; she was a short, scraggy girl, with discoloured teeth and a rough voice, who perpetually uttered vulgarities in her own slang-riddled form of English – a guttersnipe by any definition, which no doubt reflected the foreign company she had been keeping over recent years. She drove a large black car with tinted windows – the type frequently associated with *yakuza*. Being an automatic, it allowed her to drive one-handed with a leg tucked under her bottom and her free hand clutching a mobile phone that was constantly in use. Her apartment was decorated with large, thick, car tyres, an illegal antenna for a CB radio, and puddles of cats' urine on the western-style wooden floor. The table was littered with a stack of unpaid utilities bills, which explained why her home telephone and electricity were more often than not cut off.

One night, the three of us went to a cosy little *izakaya* off the main street of Tenmonkan, where, inevitably, the local *basta* situation took up a large part of the conversation. Apparently, Yumiko and Mishak had engaged some workers during a recent trip to Thailand, and were eager to restart the enterprise as they were both in need of money. Yumiko revealed, however, that her father was a police officer in Kagoshima and that it was awkward for her to continue to be seen to be connected with the local street-selling trade. I spent most of my time listening, but as the beer flowed, I could not help remarking on the arrogance of the view that this city was Mishak's territory and that it was his right to have shops here, regardless of the Japanese stalls that had increased in his absence. Despite being well aware of my potential hypocrisy, after the events in Nagasaki the previous year, I slipped easily into the role of devil's advocate.

'So, according to your Israeli law, Mishak, a foreigner, has more right to work on the street than a Japanese seller who was born here?'

'Of course he has!' exploded Budo. He was here first therefore it's his city. Remember, it is we Israelis who first brought this *basta* business to Japan. Any seller in his places must be kicked out.'

'He has no more legal right to a place on the street than anyone else, in fact, probably far less being a foreigner,' I pointed out.

'Kagoshima is Mishak's city!' they both retorted indignantly in unison. It seemed strange for a Japanese girl to be saying something so un-Japanese, but there again, she did have a vested interest. I was annoyed that their obsession with the so-called principles of Israeli street-selling made them refuse to acknowledge my legal point, and I had to vent my frustration.

'You lot really are an arrogant load of sods. There's a limit to how long the Japanese authorities will turn a blind eye to all these *basta* businesses, you mark my words.'

'Bullshit,' replied Budo. 'The police have done no more than issue warnings for years, especially in Kagoshima. It's very safe here.'

Budo's presumptuous intransigence irked me as it always did when we discussed this subject, so I left the *izakaya* ahead of them to spend some time alone. Unfortunately, I did not then realise quite how prophetic my words were to be.

★

While Budo opened his accessory shop the next day in Tenmonkan arcade, I hooked up with my old friend, Robert, to join in his football team's usual Sunday afternoon training session. I had met him in rural Kagoshima back in '89, and we had played in the same teams on and off over the next five years. He was now married to Rumi, his long-standing girlfriend from the Osumi peninsular and they were currently both working in the city. His recently formed team 'The Habu' – appropriately named after a poisonous Okinawan snake – was made up mostly of foreign English teachers. Training with them was like a nostalgic return to a former world and certainly helped to ease some of my frustrations.

That week, Budo and I travelled a little within Kagoshima Prefecture, enjoying a few of the local hot springs in the process. One night in the week, he decided to set his *basta* up in one of the main night-life buildings in Kokubu City. It was right opposite a sushi shop so we took it in turns to sample this Japanese delicacy while the other looked after the shop. The takings amounted to only Y15,000, but that really was not bad for a fairly deserted country *snaku* block on a cold winter's mid-week night.

*

Towards the end of the week we made our way back to Kumamoto. That weekend saw the first of a couple of swift returns to my old haunts in Nagasaki, partly to get a few more street experiences to add to my book material, and partly to put a little beer money in my pocket. On both of these occasions I encountered a hippie-looking Israeli individual by the name of Abner. Apparently, he had been selling in Omura and Isahaya for several months on behalf of Budo's ex-partner Zak and he was none too pleased on turning up at Dai San Royal Building to find me in his place. Fortunately for me, he was more interested in making money than trouble so he departed peacefully, though he warned me that Zak would be informed.

The second time was on a Sunday morning in front of Number 18 Bank, only this time he was not so calm, probably because Zak had ordered him to remove me physically. As he attempted to open up right next to me, I firmly took his trestles apart and put them back on his trolley, advising him to go elsewhere. He did, but only after wagging his finger at me with the news that Zak had declared war and was ready to kill to avenge the double insult carried over from the previous year. Not that I was unduly worried by this predictable threat, particularly as I had decided to go and study karate at a *dojo* of Robert's recommendation in Kagoshima.

That Sunday night, 30th March, I made arrangements to visit an Englishman called Mike in Sasebo. I had met him a few years previously when he had just come over to Japan from Thailand in order to work in the *basta* business for Budo. At that time, he had had no money, but after acquiring a Japanese wife – and therefore a right to work – he had by all accounts started to make his fortune. I was shocked at the change in him as he had ballooned to over two hundred pounds, although he did have enough height to carry it. We went to the American base with some of his friends and drank quite happily. He confided that he was depressed because he could not speak Japanese, and therefore had not made any real friends besides the soldiers who passed through. His wife confirmed his unhappy mental state and revealed that they were planning to return to England so that he could have a better quality of life.

We rounded off the night in a little *izakaya* in the centre of the city. All three of us, I thought, were in good spirits and having fun, until I stepped out of the toilet to receive three hard punches in the face from Mike's ring-adorned fists which sent me sprawling to the ground. The surprise of the attack left me momentarily stunned and speechless, but the alcohol in my system soon produced a typically violent reaction as I launched my own volley of retaliatory punches, sending him flying over the *tatami* matting, before three male staff members raced to separate us. Consequently, we spent the rest of the night in the local police station trying to explain something that was for me inexplicable. I drove back to Omura at five in the morning in my blood-spattered clothes and headed straight for Kuwa-Kuwa *onsen* where I cleansed a gash, half a centimetre deep on my arm and bathed the rest of my aching body.

A telephone call to Budo at midday revealed that Mike wanted to meet me face to face to apologise, blaming his behaviour on the drink and his depression. Identifying with the former, I agreed and he made the journey over to Omura the following day. I took no pleasure from the fact that his right eye was totally closed, since my own was a pale shade of purple, but I was glad that we were able to shake hands and put the whole thing behind us. The short return trip to Nagasaki certainly had given me something to write about, although not quite from the source that I had expected.

April/May 1997

The first Saturday in April, I attended two separate wedding parties in Kumamoto City. Both were connected to my former football team so they were fairly rowdy affairs, where I enjoyed catching up with all my Japanese friends. They were naturally curious as to whether I had decided to come back and live in Japan on a full-time basis. I filled them in on my plans to study, as well as to re-enter the teaching world at some stage in the near future.

On Monday, I returned to Kagoshima, where at around lunchtime, I went to the Guttersnipe's apartment to meet an Englishman called Malcolm, from Coventry. She had picked him up the previous day at Mizobe Airport. They had apparently met in Thailand and had arranged for him to come and sell on the streets for a while because he needed to earn some quick money for further travelling. Budo had asked me to give him a *basta* that I had brought along in his old Nissan Homy, which I was borrowing, and to explain to him the tricks of the trade. Since his sister had worked for Mishak before, he knew the basic principles of street-selling but none of the language, so I gave him a quick lesson in shop Japanese, told him the prices of the accessories, and left him to sink or swim in Kagoshima's Tenmonkan.

Over the next few days, while searching for accommodation for myself, I helped Malcolm to settle in, since the Guttersnipe had conveniently made herself unavailable. I felt sorry for him having not only to contend with the culture shock in this unfamiliar land, but also to clean his workers' apartment which had been left in a disgraceful state by the previous set of *basta* foreigners. His takings were also fairly low, which came as no great surprise since he struck me as being rather too taciturn for a salesman.

I found a modest room for myself in an old apartment block in the Kagoshima University student area of Arata. It was hardly 'all mod cons', but it was my own piece of space, and it was perfect in as much as it was excellently located for the city, without costing an arm and a leg. By this time, I had also paid my membership to join The Habu and was training regularly in the mornings with Robert, and on Sundays with the team. We had high hopes for the new season, but with an average age of over thirty, it was always going to be tough. I continued to meet up with Malcolm every now and then for a chat over lunch, and kept an eye on the money side of things. This was in accordance with Budo's request that the Guttersnipe should not get her hands on it, due to some fiasco the previous Christmas when, apparently, Y1,000,000 had mysteriously gone missing.

★

Back in Kumamoto, Budo had his car sabotaged and was convinced that he was being watched on the street of Shimotori at night, and then followed on his way home by a large black car in the early hours. At the end of April, I paid him a visit and had a rude awakening at six o'clock in the morning with the sound of shattering glass and the ear-splitting, high pitched ringing of his newly installed car alarm. We sped downstairs to discover a breeze-block lying on the back seat of his Toyota Estate and a gaping hole where the back window had been. The police arrived within half an hour but were not optimistic about catching the perpetrators, despite a teenage witness describing a large car and a group of 'Japanese Yankees'. This expression apparently defined young troublemakers, characterised by their baggy jeans, multi-pierced ears and western-looking dyed hair.

Budo was in a state of great agitation, and this reached fever pitch when two days later he awoke at a similar time to find his car on fire. Fortunately, he just managed to put it out with a garden hose before the flames reached the petrol tank. One could not help imagining what might have happened, since the vehicle was parked only three feet from his wooden house, with his wife and baby sleeping on the first floor above. The seriousness of the affair sent the local police into a fit of frenzied activity, as they installed hidden video cameras and operated round-the-clock surveillance from unmarked cars as well as from neighbouring houses. Regular patrol cars circled at night, and plain-clothed detectives kept watch from concealed positions outside, but all to no avail.

I stayed with Budo throughout this period, which was in the first fortnight of May. It brought back memories of the summer of 1994 because once again he was totally paranoid and lacking in self-confidence, assuming that the current attacks were a continuation of the never-ending battle with his ex-partner. Only reluctantly did he go to work each night, and he constantly phoned me at his home, where I had agreed to keep guard, to report on the strange faces that he was convinced were watching him.

Nothing untoward occurred until the weekend of 10th May. Frustrated at being cooped up in somebody else's house, I decided to go out on the town with Ebine san, my good friend from the football team. We enjoyed a good session as usual, after which I made my way up to Budo's stall, where he introduced me to a Mr Minami, his top ranking *yakuza* friend. We swapped business cards and had a short conversation about Budo's recent troubles, before I set off to have one for the road at a friend's bar. Some thirty minutes later, I headed back to check in on my Jewish friend, but on the way, I had an altercation with one of Zak's workers at the corner of Ginza Street.

Within seconds, Zak was on the scene, clutching his mobile phone. Out of nowhere and equally quickly appeared two *yakuza* in a large four-wheel-drive Land Cruiser. They were evidently the bosses he paid protection money to. Budo had urgently phoned Minami san in a panic, who was now walking, unhurriedly, down to the confrontation point, his sidekick reassuring us that nobody would challenge the authority of his big boss. The two sets of *yakuza* seemed surprised at the sight of each other. Minami's number two murmured to me,

'It is very bad that these two have been brought together on the street like this,' indicating Minami and the taller man with a crew-cut from the four-wheel-drive. There was an almost embarrassed reluctance on both sides to say anything, but finally there were some hurried, almost whispered exchanges between the Mafia elements, while we *gai-jin* in the group were totally ignored. Zak requested, in heavily-accented Japanese, to speak to Minami in private but he was curtly told to shut his mouth, which he obediently did. There was a tension in the air that all the night revellers in Shimotori seemed to detect as the immediate area became almost deserted.

Minami appealed for peace between Zak and Budo, suggesting that they both shake hands. Budo showed willing, but the big man turned his back. There were a few more quiet words between the Japanese Mafiosi followed by warnings to the foreigners that there should be no further trouble on the streets of Kumamoto. Then, as fast as the situation had developed, it ended, with Minami's side setting off in the direction they had come from, and the other side disappearing with a screech of tyres. Budo and I returned to his *basta*, by which point the buzz of weekend excitement had returned to the arcade as if nothing had happened.

Although neither of us had been aware of any police presence during the scene in the city centre, the fact that the authorities knew about the incident was immediately obvious on our return to Budo's house at 4.30 a.m. Police emerged from the shadows at all points of his house and reassured him that they would be on hand to deal with any trouble. There was none, but this did not help us to sleep any better.

Budo was still in an extreme state of nervousness. This only improved a few days later as a result of being summoned to Minami's office. Apparently, he drank from a special cup there and was ceremonially enrolled as a member of the family in front of the whole group. For this privilege, he would pay a fixed sum each month that would, in theory, guarantee his protection on the streets. He had never paid protection money before – it was implied that this was largely why his recent troubles had arisen – but he was only too pleased to start doing so if it would guarantee him a sound night's sleep. According to Budo, he had joked at the ceremony that he did not fancy having a finger chopped off, should he make any mistakes. Minami had seemingly laughed a long, hollow laugh.

*

Eager to put an end to my constant procrastination about learning karate, as well as actually to get my money's worth out of the room I was renting in Kagoshima, I returned to the Satsuma region in the middle of May. Robert kindly introduced me at his old *dojo* (martial arts hall) two days later, and this is where I commenced my twice weekly lessons the following Monday evening. The teachers were patient and sympathetic, while I was stiffly uncoordinated and pathetic. Nevertheless, as the great master, Kancho-sensei said, 'Ishi no ue ni mo san nen.' This old expression literally recommended that one should sit on a stone for three years, but otherwise translated meant, 'Pain and perseverance reap the finest rewards.' I certainly hoped this would be the case, anyway.

*

For the next month, my routine consisted mainly of football and karate, but I did pop along to see Malcolm every now and then. He had by this time got himself a Japanese girlfriend and seemed to be far more settled in his new way of life. Apparently, there were a lot of Japanese sellers on the streets, so he had been forced to lower his prices to be more competitive. Occasionally, the police would come along and close everybody except for the *uranai* (fortune-tellers), perfunctorily recording names, but the traders would all return to set up the following day, continuing to vend their wares as usual until the next semblance of a blitz some weeks later. According to Budo, this had been the case in most cities throughout Japan's foreign street-selling history and rarely developed into anything more serious.

12th June

At two o'clock in the afternoon I received an angry call from Budo, demanding to know why I had not answered the phone all that morning, because he needed me to go to Kagoshima's Mizobe Airport to pick up a girl arriving from Israel. I found his tone both dictatorial and offensive, so I put the phone down, telling him to call back when he had learnt some manners.

I went to the airport anyway, since I remembered the name of the girl. I knew that she was planning to work in the *basta* business and that Budo had promised to give her a place in Kagoshima's Tenmonkan. It was not difficult to find her, as there were only three foreigners in the international terminal, all sitting together. I introduced myself and discovered that the two men were also work-seeking contacts of Budo from Israel, who had coincidentally been on the same flight. Just as we were talking, there was a call on my mobile. It was Budo. He apologised for his earlier rudeness and asked if I would take all three of them back to Malcolm's apartment. He told me that he was already on the expressway and would be joining us within the hour.

Thanks to Budo's old tank of a Nissan, it was no problem to fit the three of them in with their bulky backpacks. We chatted amiably all the way back to the city, and I was impressed by their skills in English, which had always been the case in my countless previous conversations with Israelis. The girl had seemingly been in the legal profession, while the other two had recently graduated from university. Japan, for all three of them, as for so many foreigners, was intended to constitute an escape as well as the road to riches.

Budo reached the apartment towards a quarter past five. He hugged and kissed me in his typical Middle Eastern way, again apologising for the earlier misunderstanding with the excuse that he had been under pressure. I laughed it off and then watched the four of them as they discussed in Hebrew their plan of campaign. Despite their evident jet-lag, they were all keen to be initiated into the infamous Japanese *basta* business that they had heard so much about back in Israel. Budo, who had brought his own stall in the car, was eager to set up himself that night in Tenmonkan and to show the girl how the selling system worked. He asked whether I would mind taking a spare *basta* to Kokubu City, just quickly to show Rannie, the younger chap, the ropes. Not having anything better to do, and thinking that Kokubu was sufficiently rural for me not to be recognised by anybody, I agreed to open there for a couple of hours. The third Israeli was to spend the evening alongside Malcolm.

After doing the necessary introductions at Malcolm's stall in Tenmonkan, I drove the hour it took to get to Kokubu along the National Route 10 and laid out a simple stall of just two boards inside the *snaku* building where Budo had set up before. It was a quiet night and I only managed to sell three items, but still, this was enough to show Rannie how things worked. He seemed already to be fairly well informed, as his brother had done the same job for a spell in one of the larger cities on Honshu island. He also knew many of the key Japanese street-selling phrases, so I did not anticipate his encountering the communication problems that Malcolm still had.

Towards midnight, while Rannie was off making an international telephone call, I was joined by a local, larger than life individual (both physically and verbally) who, after stepping out of his dark Cadillac, demanded *basho-dai* or pitch payment and free merchandise. I managed to laugh it off with a few well-worn Japanese jokes, but could not gauge whether he was a member of the local organisation or not. Either way, everyone who passed addressed him as 'Shachou' ('Company President') and gave him an exceedingly humble bow. He was a huge fellow, weighing well over two hundred pounds, with tightly permed hair. He hung around my *basta* and continued to ask questions.

'Do you make any money here?'

'So so,' I replied vaguely.

'Bet you haven't taken anything tonight.'

'Not a lot,' I admitted, with a smile. 'Let's hope things will pick up in a minute.'

'This business is run by Jews all over Japan,' he remarked knowingly. 'Are you a Jew?'

'No, I'm not,' I answered.

'It's big business in the larger cities like Tokyo and Osaka, you know, mainly because they sell sticks as well,' he continued.

I smiled non-committally, assuming that by 'sticks' he was referring to drugs. A drunk girl staggered by arm in arm with her boyfriend and greeted me raucously. While still within earshot, the Shachou proclaimed disgustedly,

'She's not Japanese. She's a yellow cabbage.'

'A yellow cabbage?' I asked, puzzled by his metaphor.

'Yeah, she's the type of stupid young Japanese girl who goes abroad nowadays with a group of friends and is an easy lay for the locals – a cabbage lets anyone hop on top of it, you know.'

I could not help laughing at the way he said it with such a straight face when I knew full well what he was getting at.

A minute later, one of the young *snaku* bar hostesses came down from upstairs and fawned coquettishly around the *Shachou*, who seemed to be getting a kick out of it. Suddenly he called out to me,

'Give us a stick, mate.'

'Sorry, I haven't got any,' I replied calmly.

'Well, if someone like you hasn't then I don't know who has,' he bellowed. Resenting being stereotyped, my hackles rose instantly.

'Not all foreigners, let alone street-sellers are the same, you know,' I retorted defensively.

'Don't you smoke anything then?' he enquired more carefully.

'I don't even smoke cigarettes,' I answered, sounding more like a goody two shoes than I had intended.

'Oh, really?' he said, obviously not believing me.

He resumed flirting with the girl as a young man in a blazer stopped to purchase a necklace. After serving him, I turned to see the *Shachou* still sitting on a metal rail, the hostess having disappeared back upstairs.

'Fancy a beer?' he offered.

'Love to, but I'm driving,' I replied.

Apparently oblivious to my answer, he called for a pint to the sushi shop assistant, who was just returning from a delivery. Within seconds, a frosted glass of foaming lager was presented to me by the assistant who then bowed deeply to the big man.

'Ah, thank you so much,' I said awkwardly, longing for the cold yellow liquid and yet not wanting it at the same time.

'Won't you have half of it with me, Shachou san?' I asked.

He shook his head so, knowing that to refuse would have been the worst insult, I greedily downed the beer with an 'Ittadakimasu,' loving the refreshing taste despite myself and hoping that it would pass through my system by the time I came to drive home.

Rannie returned from his lengthy phone call, and after an hour or so of fruitless standing around, we packed up and returned to the city. There, the three new arrivals were taken exhausted to sleep at Malcolm's apartment. Budo and I had a couple of beers before dropping off to sleep at my place.

13th June

The next morning, I got up early to go and do some training with Robert in Hirakawa. We had an indoor five-a-side tournament that weekend which we thought we had a good chance of winning, so we needed a good workout to help us prepare. The blazing sun was already climbing high in the sky; it felt hot and humid, particularly for two Britons far more accustomed to playing the game in the middle of a European winter. We sweated profusely for an hour or so and then discussed our tactics for a while over some soft drinks, before I hopped back in the van to return home for a shower.

Budo was only just stirring, but he managed to raise himself at the prospect of a cup of coffee. We talked football for a short time before getting on to the subject of the *basta* business in Kagoshima. He said that, in his opinion, I had not spent enough time checking the condition of Malcolm's *basta*. I replied that I had not spent any time doing this, since I had no intention of getting more involved with this business than I already was, and that if he was not satisfied, he could arrange to collect the money himself. I went on to tell him about a job interview that I had attended a few weeks previously, and of my decision to start full-time teaching again by the end of the month. His reaction was explosive.

'How can you betray me like that?'

'I'm not aware that I have. I told you that I would have nothing to do with the *basta* on street level in Kagoshima. This place is part of my old world – the English-teaching world. The two just do not mix.'

'How can you go lining up other jobs without my permission? It's like you have stuck a knife in my back,' he shouted, now on his feet and waving his arms about frantically.

'Who the hell do you think you are that I have to answer to you?' I roared, now made livid by the man's arrogance. 'Let's cut our ties this minute, since you consider me on a par with Zak. I've had enough of tolerating discourteous people anyway. I suggest you pay Malcolm an extra five per cent and get him to send you the takings directly.'

'You're a stupid bastard to finish now, just as there are more workers to generate more money,' he said heatedly.

'Quality of life is more important for me, Budo. I'm going to stick to what I know in future – and that's teaching English,' I said with conviction.

There then followed a long awkward silence. Feeling uncomfortable, I broke it by suggesting that we go across to the bank so that I could withdraw Malcolm's takings which I had been looking after for him. This we did without a word, after which I unwillingly drove him to Tenmonkan to meet the girl, because he did not remember the way. She was supposed to have opened at lunchtime in the arcade, but the whole street was deserted of any form of street-seller. Even the fortune-tellers appeared to be cowering unnaturally behind convenient lamp-posts. We immediately sensed that something was wrong.

After debating what to do next, we opted to drive past Malcolm's apartment, since he was not on the phone. There was an unfamiliar, smartly-dressed official standing in the drive so we did not stop, but returned instead to my apartment. With no alternative, we sat back and waited for someone to call. Shortly before half past three the mobile rang. It was the Israeli girl. Malcolm had been arrested.

★

Budo and I, both feeling a large sense of responsibility to the newly-arrived Israelis, went by taxi to the place that the girl had indicated on the phone. Seemingly, the three of them had also been questioned but then released, though the police had informed them that they could not go back to Malcolm's apartment. We met up in a park by the river and spent the whole evening discussing what they should do – or rather I listened while the four of them debated the issue in Hebrew. They were in quite a state having been picked up by the police on only their second day in Japan. By all accounts, the police were also shocked to discover so many foreigners staying in one small flat.

Finally, it was decided that Rannie and his friend would seek work through contacts in Tokyo, while Budo would organise through a friend for the girl to work somewhere on the east coast of Kyushu. The latter two left for Kumamoto that night after Budo and I remarked with a smile of resignation upon the uncanny timing of the day's events.

I continued my own private ruminations on this point, frustrated that I had missed my first karate session since joining the *dojo*, and concerned that I could not step forward to help Malcolm without the fear of implicating myself. I resolved to leave it to fate, knowing that it would follow its own pre-determined course, anyway.

18th June

A call on my mobile in the middle of the afternoon disturbed my writing. A Japanese voice asked twice for a Nakamura san (the local equivalent of the name Smith in Britain). Apparently, it was a wrong number, though it sparked off my curiosity for two reasons: firstly, it was the first wrong number I had had on my mobile; and secondly, the fact that the caller persisted in asking again if I was Nakamura when from the outset my *gai-jin* voice obviously revealed that I wasn't – in all previous experiences in Japan, the suddenly panic-stricken caller had dropped the phone like a hot coal.

I tried to settle back down to my notes when, once again, the telephone ring interrupted my thoughts. This time, it was the Guttersnipe. Her voice, though its usual gruff self, seemed somehow strained and unnatural, emphasised by the fact that she asked me the same questions as in a previous conversation, such as where I was living exactly and what I was doing each day. Having no desire whatsoever to present the likes of her with the opportunity to drop in on me at whim, I answered evasively as before. She was eager to meet – overeager, I thought – but reluctantly accepted my excuses and hung up. I noted that during the entire dialogue she had not used a single swear-word.

My literary concentration now twice broken, I stretched out on the sofa for a snooze, half anticipating further disruptions. Even with the window open, my whole body was sticky, particularly my back and calves, which had already created a damp patch on the synthetic sofa cover. It was humid and oppressive, the whole atmosphere crying out for rain. I drifted off into a shallow doze. Later, the sound of soft padding feet in the corridor outside filtered into my slumber, quickly followed by a light tap on the door. A glance at my alarm clock revealed that it was half past five. Then there came a sharper, more urgent knock and a male voice called out,

'Luke san!'

'Hai, chotto matte, kudasai,' I replied making my way over to unlock the door. A burly, sour-faced Japanese with glasses, backed by at least four other suits, blocked the small entrance and self-importantly announced that they were the police. Even before I had finished politely inviting them in, the first two were already through the door and had taken up positions either side of me as if expecting an attempted escape or fit of violence. Despite the sudden drama, I remember automatically glancing at their feet, pleased to notice that they had removed their shoes, but painfully aware of the dirt they would inevitably be bringing in upon my twice hand-scrubbed *tatami* mats from the dusty corridor – I was not my mother's son for nothing!

The five of us made my tiny room seem ludicrously overcrowded, and I am sure I was not the only one who felt claustrophobic.

'Do you know Malcolm?' Sour-Face asked.

'Yes, I do,' I replied.

'Well, we would like you to come down to Chuo Station with us to answer some questions.'

'Hai, wakarimashita.'

They allowed me to put on some jeans and socks, the uncomfortably close proximity of these male bodies reminding me of an English Sunday-morning amateur football changing room, albeit without the friendly banter, the lascivious jokes, or the horrendous farts.

I apologised for my dishevelled and dopey appearance, pointing out that I had in fact been asleep. His automatic, 'Sumimasen ne,' while conforming to the Japanese laws of etiquette, scored no points for sincerity.

'It must be something important for all of you to come here,' I remarked.

Expressionless faces stared back at me, before the eldest one belonging to a slender policeman in his mid-fifties called Takada, cracked into a semi-friendly smile.

'You keep your room very clean and tidy.'

'I do my best,' I replied, accepting this as a genuine compliment, although I knew that it was another one of those set Japanese expressions.

After retrieving my washing through the window from the line outside, Sour-Face authoritatively ordered me to bring along my passport, business organiser, telephone and wallet. Noticing my washbag on the shelf, he instructed me to put the items in that, obviously having mistaken it for one of those male handbags that seem to be one of the Japanese man's essential accessories when he goes out for a night on the town. Pointing out that it was actually used for toiletries was to no avail.

With bag and keys in hand, I was needlessly guided by the elbow through my door into the dark wooden corridor. I noticed that my neighbour's door was closed. This was unusual, as he habitually had it wide open while sitting cross-legged on the floor and staring at the wall, wearing only his white underpants. He had doubtless run for cover at the arrival of the boys in blue. In front of the entrance to the apartment stood a younger detective acting as sentry. I greeted him with as gusty a 'Konnichiwa' as I could muster under the circumstances which seemed momentarily to send his ever so serious demeanour into a fluster, apparently not quite sure whether he ought to reply or not. However, in the end, he did manage a grunt.

As I was led over to two waiting cars, yet more senior suits appeared, seemingly from out of the bushes. I was steered into the back seat of a grey saloon, flanked on either side by a senior detective, and then we set off in convoy through the city to the police station. Even with the car's air-conditioning, I was sweating profusely and, though I tried to control the nervous shaking in my legs, I sensed that the Japanese equivalent of Bodie and Doyle could feel it and were enjoying it.

Chuo Police Station was a shabby, faceless building just off the tram line, not far from Tenmonkan, the principal street in Kagoshima City. I was led through the main reception area, up a flight of stairs and into a tiny room on the third floor. An unsmiling, youthful-looking detective ordered me to sit down and seated himself the other side of a scruffy desk.

'Kimi wa jubbun asondekita ne,' he commented bluntly.

I did not appreciate being 'kimied' at the best of times, for it was an overly casual form of address, yet to be 'kimied' and told that for me the good life was over both in the same sentence by a stranger, who had not even had the manners to introduce himself, was more than a little irritating. I made a point of drawing attention to his lack of courtesy by being over-polite myself in my reply, using the honorific term of address.

'O-taku mo... I am sure you too have enjoyed your share of sport, beer and karaoke bars, haven't you?'

'Um, so ne,' he responded rather awkwardly.

At this point, the elder, slender detective reappeared. His junior made way for him so that he could sit directly opposite me. Then the questioning began. Firstly, they wanted to know all about my history in Japan right from its beginning. I pointed out that it would be easier for them to refer to my passport, as it contained all my entry and exit stamps, as well as the numerous teaching visa stamps. This they attempted to do but predictably failed to comprehend much at all, so I had to write its contents out in chronological order on a separate piece of paper. They suspected that my passport was false and ran it through a check, pointing out that there were one hundred and twenty-five thousand illegal immigrants in Japan.

After questioning me about the purpose of my visit, in my description of which I detailed my friend's wedding, karate and a possible future teaching job, Takada finally got around to Malcolm. Up to this point, I had been answering mainly in Japanese, only occasionally humouring the 'Kimi'-merchant when he insisted on unnecessarily translating the simple bits into English for me. The last of those occasions came on the subject of my relationship with the Guttersnipe, after I had explained that I had first met Malcolm through her.

'How long have you been friends?' asked Takada.

'She is merely an acquaintance,' I replied in English.

'He met her three days ago in her apartment,' he translated.

I immediately retranslated it, noting, with not a little relish, the 'Kimi'-merchant's loss of face, and resolved to field all future questions as best I could in the foreign tongue. If I were eventually to be hanged, it might as well be due to my own linguistic shortcomings and not due to somebody else's incompetence.

I continued to explain that I had met her through my good friend Mr Goldstein who, like Malcolm, ran a *rotensho* business in Kumamoto City, except that he had a working visa and operated with what seemed to be the full approval of the local police and tax authorities. I pointed out that having known Mr Goldstein for a number of years I was familiar with his work, and had thus been in a position to give Malcolm, a fellow Englishman, a few tips after his arrival in this alien land.

Takada listened to this explanation with the beginnings of an omniscient smile creeping on to his face. Suspecting something far more sinister behind all this, he opened his attack.

'I think you're involved in all this Kyushu street-selling business – probably a boss.'

I laughed scornfully. 'You obviously aren't very well informed about this business, Mr Takada. Didn't you know that it is dominated by Israelis? An Englishman like myself would not get a look in.'

'Well, perhaps you're somebody's messenger-boy then,' piped up the other one.

'I don't know what you mean,' I replied, unable to disguise my annoyance at being given such a piffling title, as well as at his sarcastic tone. 'By the way, I know this is Mr Takada but I don't know your name.

'I'm Tomo Suzuki,' he said in English.

Making a written note, I resolved that this particular character would definitely be getting a few very special pages devoted to him in the not too distant future. It turned out that he also spoke a certain amount of Spanish, as a result of a two year study spell in the States.

They continued to question me in the same vein for the next three hours insinuating that I was covering something up. I repeatedly gave them the same answers, insisting that Malcolm was merely a friend whom I'd helped on various occasions and nothing more. It was not until eleven at night that they finally terminated the interview. The three of us signed the statement, I with a paw print and the other two with their personal seals. I couldn't help smirking when Detective Suzuki gave himself the rather exotic title of translator, making me feel that I ought to have been entitled to put His Royal Highness in front of my name at the very least.

23rd June

It was nine o'clock in the morning and my friend Richard had just left for Shibushi. He had come up the previous day to attend a teachers' meeting after which we had indulged in a few beers together at a local *izakaya*. I was absent-mindedly watching television, when there came a tap on the door immediately followed by the sudden invasion of the previous week's police crew. A short senior detective with glasses produced an arrest warrant in English and awkwardly spat out an accompanying phrase to inform me that my room was about to be searched. I voiced my disapproval but knew that I could do nothing sensible to prevent it, so I merely sat on my love-sofa and resentfully observed the proceedings.

Two of the detectives donned white gloves and half-heartedly scrutinised the contents of the few boxes of miscellaneous junk stored under my futon closet. Another went through the pockets of my clothes in the other cupboard while a fourth rifled through my personal correspondence. Takada stood and stared in arrogant silence. At one point, the rubbish-sifters did get mildly excited over a photograph of me surrounded by a group of foreigners. It provoked a number of questions, but proved to depict nothing more sinister than a scrappy game of Sunday afternoon football. On discovering that the other six albums contained more of the same, they moved on to the next box.

After twenty minutes, in which their efforts had produced nothing of note, one detective commented that they were 'scrunching up their buttocks after letting a fart,' or less literally translated, were attempting to shut the door when the horse had already bolted. Very astute, I thought, bearing in mind that today's warrant came almost one week after my initial questioning and a full eleven days after

Malcolm's very public arrest. Nobody with prior knowledge of an imminent police swoop is likely to dwell so long on any piles of incriminating evidence.

I was instructed to pack my diary, letters, bank-books and other identity papers into my toilet bag as before. Then I was once again frog-marched out to two waiting cars, handcuffed and bundled into the back of one of them, sandwiched between detectives as before. Despite the escalating gravity of my situation, I felt relieved that their perfunctory search had failed to unearth the ¥200,000 under the baseball cap on my wall. I had cleared out my Higo Bank account the previous Monday in anticipation of the Kagoshima police pursuing this investigative charade and freezing my private assets in the process.

Our ride along the busy tram route was taken in blazing sunshine, but the momentary brightness of the day was all too soon replaced by the depressing austerity of Chuo Police Station. As I got out of the car my handcuffs were checked, and I was then guided into the dark building, through the main reception, up a flight of stairs, along a labyrinth of corridors and into a large third floor office. I had not been brought this far on my previous visit, but deduced from the desk arrangement that it was normally occupied by up to a score of detectives, of whom apparently the majority were now awaiting my arrival in expectant but silent Japanese poker-faced fashion, with evidently nothing more pressing to attend to. I was made to sit down at one of the end desks whereupon my cuffs were undone and I was tied to my chair with a length of cord. Never having been treated like a common criminal before in my life, I found such a precaution melodramatic bordering on farcical, rather than seeing it as an act of their professionalism. This served merely to fuel my indignation.

The arrest paper was once more produced and I was invited to read it at my leisure so as to fully comprehend the charges. It consisted of a short paragraph stating that I had employed a certain Malcolm Laurel, whose visa status was that of 'Temporary Visitor', to vend accessories in Kagoshima's Tenmonkan district between April and June of this year. The overriding tone of the passage was that I was responsible for bringing him to Japan to sell for me, effectively making me the boss of this business. I strongly resented the charges. Still on my dignity, I spent the next ten minutes pedantically highlighting at least eight spelling mistakes in the document and derived a perverse pleasure from watching the grey little official run backwards and forwards to his electronic typewriter to dutifully amend them. On the fourth attempt, I condescendingly conceded that the piece was at last legible. This was when Takada avenged the colleague who had had to do all the corrections, by informing me that I would be investigated thoroughly for the rest of the day and that I would not be going home.

★

I felt like Elephant Man as I was led through the various offices accommodating the numerous sections making up the Chuo Police Headquarters. Everybody paused from their work to look up, and it seemed almost as if I was being paraded as some kind of sporting trophy or figure of fun. Being manacled and roped in front of all these Japanese was deeply humiliating and my face was set in deep anger, not to mention acute embarrassment. We went down several flights of stairs before we came to a locked iron door. This was opened from the inside and I was then handed over to three stout guards in light blue uniform. The accompanying detectives came no further. This marked my transfer to Japan's equivalent of Her Majesty's Prison.

Once inside a tiny room no more than three feet wide, the last of the three guards filed in behind me and locked the door. There was a narrow table against the wall, upon which I was told to lay down the contents of my pockets. I then had to surrender my belt, followed by my jeans. Underneath I was wearing cut-off Adidas tracksuit bottoms but could not manage to remove the waistband cord as requested.

'Haven't you brought a spare pair of pants?' asked a guard.

'It is not something I am in the habit of carrying around with me,' I replied.

'Well, you should have brought a change of clothes with you, shouldn't you? Anyway, you'll have to take them off and we'll lend you a pair of trunks,' he said.

I was not exactly enamoured with the prospect of stepping into a pair of prison communal underwear, but since my captors had failed to inform me of His Emperor's house rules at the moment of my arrest, I had no choice but to bow to his magnanimity. Bashfully, I slipped into the proffered pale blue boxer shorts under the constant gaze of the guards. I was then allowed to put my jeans back on, to sign for my possessions and to be led out the other side of the small room, where my handcuffs were unlocked. All of a sudden, one of the guards let out the loud exclamation, 'He's still wearing his watch!'

'And his ring!' observed the fattest of the three.

I was then led hurriedly back into the tiny room where, with more than a shade of embarrassment at such a basic oversight, the guards relieved me of these last two items. The watch did not matter but my cornelian ring was of enormous sentimental value to me. Before handing it over, I made a mental note of the senior warden's name, 'Honda san', informing him that I would hold him personally responsible for its safe return. I was deadly serious.

Honda san then led me past a line of cells which were positioned in a semicircle around a central arc of washbasins with a guard-tower observer point on the first floor above. I heard the murmur of 'Gai-jin' as I passed, and the comment that I was a different foreigner to the previous detainee was clearly audible. My cell was Number One. I stepped backwards out of the plastic green slippers I had just been given directly up onto the elevated *tatami* of my room. Unfortunately, I had failed to take into account the unnaturally small dimensions of the entrance – as well as having the desire to retain my dignity by staying erect – therefore I cracked the top of my head with full force on the horizontal metal door frame. I felt instantly nauseated and hardly heard Honda san close the door after me.

It took me some minutes to recover, and then some more to take in my new surroundings, which were even sparser than my memories of Clint Eastwood's Alcatraz: three bare dirty grey *tatami* mats cut to fit the irregular curving shape of the inner wall; a see-through cubicle with a Japanese-style toilet to the rear; roughly-painted light green walls on two sides; wire-meshed doors with iron bars stood at both ends of the room and a high, white-painted ceiling with a metal grill covering its bar light. The sole concession to human comfort was an old blanket folded up in the corner. Like the *tatami*, it was covered with long brown hairs. They were obviously Malcolm's, yet far from considering them a comfort, I found them absolutely disgusting.

Within minutes, grey metal bowls were being distributed through the meal hatches at the base of the cell doors. It was just midday, which according to the daily prison timetable I had been shown while changing, was the appointed hour for lunch. Today was green tea, dried pickles, *miso* soup, rice and fishcakes. I had certainly eaten far worse. After gulping it down greedily I put the empty vessels outside the hatch, and hearing all the other prisoners express their thanks on collection with the ritual 'Gochisosama deshita', I naturally followed suit. There were two sets of dishes outside the other cells which indicated that these cells were designed for two people. I prayed that nobody else would be put in with me – it would be hard enough taking a crap in full public display, let alone with the audience sitting right alongside. I shuddered, settled back on an apparently hairless space, and tried to think of England.

Not long after, the rattling of the key in my door told me that I was on the move again. Honda san explained to me that it was time for 'O-shirabe' otherwise known as investigative interview. He put me back in the handcuffs and led me through the tiny room by the length of cord, then passed me over to the waiting detectives the other side, Takada and a younger, more open looking individual called Yamazaki. I was led once again like a circus animal all the way through the police departmental offices, through the large room where I had been before lunch and into a smaller room, where I was once more tied elaborately to my chair, the cuffs having been unlocked and stuffed into my pocket. The door was left open so I could see virtually all twenty of the morning's detectives going through the personal effects that they had seized from me, and smiled as I tried to imagine any other human being, let alone a Japanese, attempting to decipher my mother's rather unique handwriting. As it was, a young stern-faced detective at the nearest desk was poring over my diary with a dictionary – a complete waste of time since I used my own ironic brand of shorthand and had long-since mailed all my literary accounts of street-selling to a trusted friend on the Osumi peninsular.

Detective Takada went over the same ground as he had already covered on our previous encounter, only this time, he laboriously typed it up on his electronic typewriter. I co-operated by fielding all the questions as best I could in Japanese, and any technical language that I could not understand was patiently put more simply by one of them. I denied being Malcolm's boss and stuck to the explanation that I had merely helped him with his business along the way. Takada was convinced that I was lying, but despite one or two verbal explosions of frustration, dutifully typed up my version of events. Shortly before five o'clock I was returned to my cell for supper, before being investigated again until seven o' clock.

Bedtime at eight o'clock came as a relief. We went in turn to get our futons and bedding from a storeroom, and after I had washed quickly with borrowed soap and cleaned my teeth with my index finger, I lay down. Lights-out was an hour later, but it was some time before I could get off to sleep because my brain was still racing from the day's bombardment of questions. My pillow, which was more akin to an aeroplane armrest in shape, was as hard as a paving slab.

24th June

I awoke to the sound of echoing footsteps on the concrete floor and a broom being shoved through my meal flap. It took me a few moments to get my bearings because, as clichéd as it might sound, I really did believe that I was just coming to the end of a bad dream. The stark reality of my confined surroundings came as a nasty shock. This was brought home to me all the more when the lights came on at six thirty and a loud voice instructed me to sweep my cell and put my bed away before wiping the floor over with a damp cloth. A soiled rag which stank of excrement was provided for the toilet area, so I cleaned everything as best I could, in accordance with the oft-cited characteristics of the typical home-loving Cancerian.

We then took turns to wash in the sinks opposite the cell doors. For the first time, I started to take in the types around me. With me on the ground floor were about a dozen others, all falling between the ages of twenty and forty, except for one old man who had to be well into his sixties. About half of them were heavily tattooed, which indicated only one thing; but the atmosphere was not in any way intimidating. Actually, it was very civilised, as most inmates greeted each other in the morning just as they had done the previous night. A couple of the younger ones even tried to strike up a conversation in English, though they soon switched to Japanese when getting down to the more serious question of why I was in there. I joked that I had been pulled in for selling my body in soapland, which seemed to go down well, even though they continued to speculate as to whether I was involved with Malcolm.

Around seven o'clock, eight of us were led upstairs past the watch tower and along the back passage of an equal number of first-floor cells out into an open roof-yard. It was no more than about eighteen feet by thirty-five surrounded by high walls covered with wire fences – an exceedingly small area for *Taiso no jikan* or 'exercise period', I thought. Nevertheless, it was good to breathe some fresh air and enjoy the relatively less polluted environment of the upper sections which surrounded Kagoshima's high-rise flats and offices. I spent the short fifteen minutes pacing the width of the yard at the far end, while the other seven sat on their haunches in a circle by the guard at the entrance, all drawing heavily on cigarettes. Intermittently, they would glance across and make reference to the *gai-jin*, but not in a malicious way. I was conscious that perhaps they might see my not joining them as aloofness, when in reality it was merely the smoke at such an early hour that I found offensive.

As we filed back in, I chatted to a younger inmate. Apparently, he had been in here for a few months because his case – stealing Y5,000,000 – was still being investigated. I concluded that to all intents and purposes this place, though on a small scale, resembled a full-blown gaol rather than just a custody house, although with no point of comparison, it was difficult to tell. He paused to greet a goat-bearded young man respectfully through the back of a cell, as had all the others before us. I also said, 'hello' but he just seemed to stare back at me coldly.

Breakfast consisted of more rice, *miso* soup and dried pickles. After this, a group of guards came around led by a very short middle-aged man with slicked back hair who bellowed, 'Ken-ba!' Not familiar with this particular expression, I continued to sit on my *tatami* mat. For some reason, this angered the man and he screamed at me to stand up and show some respect to my superiors. I did so, and was instantly ordered out of the cell so that he could enter. He removed his highly polished shoes and, without having to bend much at all, stepped backwards up onto the *tatami*. From the way he banged every corner of my empty room and searched even in the toilet hole, I gathered that this new piece of vocabulary meant 'room inspection'. Content that there were no concealed weapons in my previously neatly folded blanket, he stepped back down into his built-up shoes and moved to the neighbouring cell.

By now, shaving was in full swing around by the lockers outside the back of the cells. Two rotor-head electric razors and small mirrors had been set out by a guard, and he supervised the prisoners as they were called out in pairs. Being a wet-and-dry man and not particularly fancying direct contact with other people's facial germs, I declined the experience, though I feared that the longer I was in here, the less fussy I would have to become. At one point, two Filipino girls were led down from the first floor to take a turn on the shaving equipment. Although I could not see them, the mind boggled, until I concluded that they must be transvestites.

At eight o'clock, everybody was allowed to go to their lockers and get their current reading matter, writing materials, or snacks. The snacks, apparently, you could order a day in advance every other day from a guard who would come around towards lunchtime with a clipboard. The books you could request throughout the day after selecting from a list on the cell wall, assuming you could read the Japanese titles that is. I asked the guard for anything in English and he promised to have a look, despite there being nothing on the list. I also took the opportunity to point out politely that I did not yet have a toothbrush or my own soap, and he said he would get on to this too.

Since, for some reason or other, I was not permitted writing materials, and I had nothing to read, I could only lie back with my hands behind my head. Fortunately, before long I was called for investigation, which for all its negative points, helped keep the brain active, as well as providing me with a free Japanese language lesson.

*

Instead of being handed over to Detective Takada and his colleagues today, I was taken charge of by a different set of uniformed police who were responsible for transporting those in custody between Chuo Prison and the chief prosecutor's office downtown. Four of us were escorted in handcuffs by minibus across the busy city centre. Even though I had only been locked up for one night, the bustling, free way of life outside seemed to be part of a totally different world. I already felt nostalgic.

The prosecutor's office was in another drab building, though the interior was certainly a lot plusher than the police station. We were locked in a waiting room with an armful of pornographic magazines, and led upstairs individually at intervals to have our cases heard. I was the last to go.

The chief prosecutor was an exceedingly small man even by Asian standards, though his diminutive proportions were not immediately obvious because he was seated on a raised swivel chair. I was tied to a chair opposite him. To his right was an interpreter called Mr Keshima, whose face I recalled vaguely from the English teaching world, and in front of him was a bespectacled young man on a word processor. The prosecutor did not appear to be in the best of moods as he finished chastising the young man for his clumsiness on the keyboard and then turned his brusque manner on me. He barked out an instruction for me to give my name. His rudeness, exacerbating my mounting frustration at being caught up in a legal system that I did not understand and that nobody had seen fit to explain, irked me. After giving my name, I asked if he might be kind enough to introduce himself, thinking that it would be useful to have his name for future reference.

He instantly exploded, 'Kimi ni aisatsu suru hitsuyou ga nai!' ('I don't have to introduce myself to somebody like you'). It was that 'Kimi' word again which made my hackles rise and put me back on my dignity.

'Chijin naka ni mo reigi ari,' I quoted, tailoring a well-known Japanese proverb to emphasise the importance of good manners in all situations.

Switching to English, I then added rather pompously, 'It is when we lose our manners that we are in danger of becoming machines.'

I glanced across at Mr Keshima to see him squirming with discomfort, but nonetheless, he translated it with a nervous laugh. The prosecutor, however, did not appreciate the condescension tables being turned upon him.

'Who cares what you think? I don't have to justify my manners to you,' he screamed at me.

'Oh, but that's where you're wrong. I think I could give you a very good lesson in courtesy,' I continued, unable to stop the flow.

Had Mr Keshima been able to disappear up one of his own orifices, I am convinced he would have done so, but not being blessed with that option he paused to consider the best way to translate it. The momentary gap allowed me to see the foolhardiness of pursuing this course, since the individual I was riling held my fate in his hands, so I quickly told Keshima san to forget my last sentence. He did as I said with great relief.

After informing me of my right to remain silent, the prosecutor went through what was obviously Takada's report of the case, asked me various questions and then proceeded to dictate a summary of it all for the official on the word processor. A separate monitor in front of the prosecutor simultaneously displayed the text and at regular intervals he would yell criticism at the poor fellow for his inefficiency, although, to me, he seemed to be working flat out. I was not the only one to feel sorry for him.

I was able to answer most of the questions honestly, except the part about Malcolm's takings. Even though I was not under oath, I felt uncomfortable about having to lie that I knew nothing about the financial side of his enterprise, but this was the crux of the whole case. Budo and I had resolved to stick to the story that none of us were connected with the business, assuming that without any proof, the police would not have a case against us. Revealing anything about the money would lead the police directly to Budo's door, and would definitely open up a whole new can of worms. Not for the first time, I cursed the fact that I had to consider anyone else besides myself.

Last of all, the prosecutor asked me if I had any comments to make. I said that I hoped that my case would be put in its correct context. In other words, I wanted it to be judged against the background of the whole nationwide phenomenon of street-selling, and more particularly, in relation to its ten year history in Kagoshima City. After all, I had only been in the city for a few months and had no intention of being held responsible for the last decade.

It took some while for Mr Keshima to translate these points satisfactorily in Japanese, and when we went back over the text, I became aware of a gap in the translations which bothered me. The prosecutor was getting more and more frustrated about the time the retranslations were taking. He continually tutted, sighed and scowled as he impatiently eyed the clock on the wall, and was on the verge of another eruption when I said the text would do, and reluctantly put my fingerprint to it.

I politely thanked the prosecutor for his time, Mr Keshima for his translations, and the young man for recording the minutes. As the guard released me from the chair and slipped on my handcuffs, I glanced across at the little prosecutor. He was whirling around on his chair, both feet a full thirty centimetres off the floor, as if he were on his own private merry-go-round.

*

We were all returned to our cells for lunch before being shuttled straight back again. I was escorted to a video room where I was shown a film in English about the Japanese judicial process. This was very enlightening, since my knowledge on this subject was close to non-existent, and Detective Inspector Takada and his colleagues had not bothered to inform me of my rights, if indeed I had any. It certainly explained today's trip to the prosecutor's office, because apparently, under Japanese law, the police could only detain a suspect for forty-eight hours before passing their findings on to the prosecutor, who would then determine – on the police's recommendation – if the suspect should continue to be held or not. If he was held, the subsequent custodial periods came in two ten-day blocks, at the end of which either a fine or gaol sentence would be decided upon. This did not take into account why our resident multi-million-yen thief was still being held in custody and investigated daily after several months. I concluded that it was better not to dwell on this thought.

Shortly before four o'clock, I was led into a simply furnished room and told to sit and wait for today's judgement. Within minutes, two men in suits arrived with a woman. The younger man, probably in his late thirties and with the demeanour of a cold fish, addressed me through the female interpreter. He informed me curtly that I was to be detained for another ten days while the police carried out further enquiries. During that time, I could see no one but a lawyer, whom I could hire at my own expense, after a first consultation which would be free. The British Embassy would apparently be informed if I so wished.

My first thoughts were for my mother, who would be frantic with worry if some faceless voice from the consulate informed her of my predicament over the telephone. To make matters worse, I knew she would be calling me on my birthday, in six days' time. I had to contact her, but my request for one telephone call was denied.

This prompted me to ask the Cold Fish, 'Have you got a mother?'

He looked to the interpreter uncomprehendingly, though it was inconceivable that an individual in his position could not understand such basic English, even in

Japan. She translated it awkwardly, but the official remained impassive. He passed on to the next matter which was to ask me if I had any comments I wished to make. I basically reiterated my morning statement, stressing how ludicrous it was that I was being charged as the boss of a business which had been established almost a decade before my arrival in the city. Yet again, the translation of my argument about the necessity of putting this case in its correct context was abysmal, so I translated it myself to put the point across adequately.

The younger official failed to sum up my comments to my satisfaction, so for the second time that day, I had to resign myself to the linguistic gap. Finally, I made my decision to decline the offer to inform the embassy but to take advantage of the lawyer. After all, with another ten days inside, things were looking a bit serious. In fact, I suspected that the outcome had already been predetermined. I was a very convenient scapegoat for a police force which needed to make an example of someone in order to give the message to a foreign street-selling industry that it had been allowed to thrive for too long. It was with these thoughts that I sat in silence on the way back to prison, convinced that the afternoon's Cold Fish had not got a father either.

*

No sooner was I back in my cell than I was fetched by one of the guards and escorted to a room upstairs. Apparently the lawyer had arrived. He was seated behind an opaque screen. I introduced myself and thanked him for coming so promptly. He told me that his name was Sato and that he was a friend of the Tsuruta family, who were also friends of mine. At the time I dismissed this as coincidence, but later discovered that it was Japan's inner wheels at work.

Sato san had brought with him a cutting from the local Minami-Nihon Newspaper, detailing my arrest and depicting me as the brains behind the whole street-selling racket. He asked me directly if it was true. I told him truthfully that I had some part in it but that both the newspaper article and the police allegations were a gross exaggeration. Sato san went on to explain Japan's judicial procedure and speculated, on the basis of what I had said, that in a small case such as this, I could expect to be released with a fine after ten or twenty days. If however, my involvement was proved to be greater, the case could go to trial, and that could lead to a prison sentence. I asked Sato san what I should do with regard to hiring a lawyer. He advised me not to bother because the cost would far outweigh the benefits. I took this as a positive sign and really appreciated his candour. After enlisting Mr Sato's help to communicate to Robert the need to put my mother's mind at rest, I thanked him profusely for his time and returned to my cell.

*

During the course of the evening I asked the younger, friendly guard called Hamadome san about the book situation. He told me he was still making enquiries, but that in the meantime, I could have a look at some simple Japanese comic-type books. Anything would be better than nothing – or so I thought until I read the story about two bears eating a sow and then proving to her distraught piglet that they were not the culprits by taking a diarrhoea-laden crap saying, 'Told you it wasn't us.'

Bedtime came as a relief. I asked an obese older guard with a crew-cut about my toothbrush. Not for the first time, he ignored me and continued barking orders in his incomprehensible Kagoshima *ben* (local dialect) to another prisoner. I gave him a moment to finish and then tried again in perfectly polite standard Japanese.

He stared back aggressively. 'Nan ya?'

I repeated myself for a third time, but still unable to understand, he looked helplessly to a Japanese inmate, who obliged with a Kagoshima *ben* translation of my question. By now, a few of the others were sniggering at the oaf's inability to understand his own language, which enraged him even more. He hissed at me to shut up and get on with my wash, grumbling to another guard about the impudence of 'the bloody Gai-jin'. The temptation to confuse him further with his own tongue was strong, but I settled for exploring my dental crevices with my finger, whilst mentally nicknaming him, 'The Peasant'.

I overheard two of the other prisoners commenting, 'Kokusai-teki ni natte kita ne,' meaning that my presence lent an international air to this country establishment.

Hamadome san's announcement as he closed the door to my cell, that there were no books in any European language, not even a Bible, led me to the swift conclusion that the only thing 'kokusai-teki' about the place was me.

26th June

The previous day had been unremarkable except for two minor events; I had enjoyed my first of two weekly baths, and later, at the police record centre, I had measured in at all of a hundred and eighty-one centimetres – a full half inch taller than usual thanks, no doubt, to the egg-shaped lump on the top of my head. Other than this, there had been little investigating, probably because the police had secured at least another ten days of my company.

This morning, Detectives Takada and Yamazaki turned up to collect me a little after half past nine. As I was led along the usual route of corridors and departmental offices, Takada enquired formally about the food, while his junior casually practised his English with a big smile on his face. Once in the poky interview room, Yamazaki san kindly got me a cup of coffee. Takada set up his typewriter and informed me that as usual, they would conduct the interview in Japanese, but that an interpreter would come in later to check any differences in nuance with me. He urged me to help myself by being honest, because then he could help me too. He also pointed out that they had a lot of information from various sources, which included a comprehensive diary written by Malcolm with my name written throughout.

The entire day was spent questioning me on my financial situation since entering Japan at the end of February. I had kept most of the money I had brought over with me in cash and had largely lived off this for the first three months. Fortunately, I had not opened my Kagoshima Bank account until the end of May, but it was unfortunate that I had deposited some of Malcolm's profits there before passing them on to Budo. Revealing this would have saved me the headache of trying to cover up the various transactions with feasible explanations, but I was determined not to disclose Budo's involvement. I had to account for every deposit and every withdrawal, remembering the dates and reasons for each. Unlike the detectives outside, I did not have the benefit of my bank book for reference, and I was painfully aware that my figures had to tally. It also occurred to me that these amounts would also be checked against any information Malcolm had given and could eventually be cross-referenced with Budo's bank book. I genuinely could not recall everything, and I told Takada so. As my frustration mounted, he was close to boiling point.

'You writhe and wriggle like an eel with your vague answers, don't you?' he observed hotly.

'Have you ever tried to remember exactly how much and on precisely which day of the week you drew out a sum from your cashpoint the previous month? I bet you couldn't!' I replied angrily.

'You shouldn't have so much trouble if you tell the truth,' he fired back.

Well, you're not entirely wrong there, I thought to myself.

Three cups of coffee and eight hours later, I was returned to my cell for the day. My head was throbbing and all I could do was pace up and down the short length of my room going over the day's calculations, as well as trying to anticipate the next day's awkward questions. I noticed that the window in the corridor at the back of the cell was open for the first time. When I craned my neck, I could just see out on to the busy main road and spotted a *tako-yaki* (grilled octopus) take-away shop in the distance, with a single customer. During the next two hours of pacing, regular glances at that slice of life from the real world nearly always showed one customer being served. On a daily basis, this made a very steady flow of business indeed. Had I not been in this gaol, I would never have known quite what a little gold-mine *tako-yaki* was.

29th June

With the arrival of the weekend, I had hoped that the police would take time off like normal citizens, but if anything, they doubled their investigative efforts. Earlier in the week, on the subject of my involvement with Malcolm, I had constantly appealed for my statements to be put in their correct contexts, instead of reported in loaded police jargon as a bare list of street-selling-related activities. Now they had gone to the opposite extreme in their sudden desire to supply some background, since Detective Inspector Takada had taken it into his head to chart my daily movements for the previous four months of my life.

Remembering precisely what you have done for the last hundred and twenty days during an unspectacular period in your life is no easy feat, and had I not had my regular karate and footballing sessions to use as a point of reference, I would have failed more miserably than I did. More annoying still was that other detectives were apparently making regular enquiries through Robert, so whenever my memory did not exactly match his, Takada automatically assumed that I was lying which, as far as any of my activities with Robert were concerned, there was absolutely no reason to do.

Detective Yamazaki, who had more of your friendly local village bobby about him, was visibly pained when I could not recall everything in as much minute detail as Takada was unreasonably demanding. He constantly gave me subtle hints to jog my memory, sometimes to the extent that it caused friction with his older more urbane superior. His presence, and frequent cups of coffee are probably what prevented Takada and me from throwing one another out of the window, particularly when Takada unfairly equated my frequent use of the Japanese verb 'omou' (to think) with being indefinite and evasive. For anybody familiar with the Japanese language, it is a well-known fact that *omou* is greatly overused as a softening expression, to the extent that even a mayor giving a speech will usually open by telling his audience what he *thinks* he is going to talk about. I pointed out this linguistic trait, unable also to resist defining 'think' as a word used to express uncertainty, which is exactly what I felt when asked to state precisely what time I ate my lunch on Saturday, 2nd March, 1997. The detective inspector just smirked knowingly at me.

As each fresh page of my statement rolled off the electronic typewriter the whole department, waiting eagerly outside, greedily gathered it up and cross-checked it with all their other information. I found it truly incredible that the Kagoshima police force were willing to devote so many man-hours to a case revolving around somebody selling a pendant on a street, especially since it was happening the full length of the country and had been for many years. Nonetheless, I had to give them full marks for being thorough.

Up to this weekend, my biggest problem, besides having to avoid implicating Budo, was not knowing exactly how much the police actually knew and could prove. Therefore, apart from confessing to helping Malcolm with his business as a friend, I had consistently denied involvement on a deeper level. It was only that afternoon that I began to realise the futility of pretence and altruistic protective motives when Takada revealed that the number plate of Budo's van, which I had been using for the duration, had popped up at regular intervals on hidden cameras scattered all over the region. It therefore followed that such cameras existed nationwide, so I decided the time had come to tell them about my selling activities in Nagasaki Prefecture to fill in a little more of that crucial background. They seemed neither surprised nor bothered by this, but asked my motive for deserting the respectable world of teaching for the stigmatised life on the streets. My answer that I wanted to use the experience as material for a book was met with derision and was one of the many background truths not to make it onto Takada's printer.

Even though I insisted that my selling in Nagasaki had never been part of a business arrangement with Budo, the police felt otherwise and this gave Takada a new focus for his attack. He was determined to flush out anybody behind the scenes connected with Malcolm, and now that Budo's name and his van fitted so conveniently into the equation, there would be no deterring him from his new line of questioning.

I was returned to my cell that night feeling totally drained.

The short Mr Kenba was on duty and as he relieved me of my handcuffs commented, 'You're pretty tall, aren't you?'

He then drew himself up to his full five feet two inches and revised his opinion to 'taishita koto nai,' meaning that my height was not anything to write home about.

I plodded silently back to my room and stared at the steady comings and goings at the *tako-yaki* shop.

Shortly before bedtime, a mild-mannered guard by the name of Yoshinaga san quietly handed me two paperbacks. One was a biography of a golfer – of all things – and the other was a Michael Crichton novel. They both still had their price labels on, suggesting that somebody had just been out to buy them. If I thanked Mr Yoshinaga once, I thanked him ten times, bowing in equally extravagant quantities. Never had I imagined that I would be so grateful to receive the life story of somebody of the profession of Tiger Woods. This moment of elation was only partially destroyed at wash-time by a sharp slap in the kidneys from Kenba. Apparently, it was against the rules to strip to the waist; we were expected to wash our armpits through our T-shirts. I did not bother pointing out that nobody had objected up until then, but simply put it down to the insecurity of an inconsequential human being.

30th June

The highlight of this particular day was the sight of a graceful hawk during the morning exercise period. I was the only one to witness this ultimate symbol of freedom as the others were all filling their lungs with smoke, as usual. Towards the end of the fifteen minute period, I talked to a pleasant young lad called Kurumade. Apparently, he was doing his stretch for grievous bodily harm, as he had battered some poor chap half to death after a heavy drinking session. He did not expect to be released for quite some time, but speculated that I was sure to be let out soon. Nevertheless, he was unable to explain why most of the other prisoners were allowed to order sweet snacks and have access to writing materials, whilst my pleasures were restricted to sliced bread and my golf book.

The day-long interview with Takada merely outlined the impossibility of my situation. Malcolm had, in order to secure his own freedom, sung like the proverbial nightingale and, to cap it all, the Guttersnipe had signed sworn statements against Budo and myself to the effect that we were running the Kagoshima business. I considered the strong possibility that I was merely being tricked into submission, but the evidence of their intimate knowledge of even the tiniest details about the source of Malcolm's *basta* materials filled me with foreboding. The tactless spectacle that afternoon of the Guttersnipe flitting as freely as the morning's hawk around the neighbouring office, when I was tied to my seat in the interview room was the absolute limit. Having heard her distinctive gruff tones through the open door and watched her pouring tea with a laugh for all her father's detective colleagues, I demanded to know what sort of a cover-up they were engineering. Takada hastily closed the door with his first and only look of complete embarrassment, while Yamazaki shuffled uncomfortably in his chair, attempting to smooth things over with the comment, 'Oh, you don't want to worry about her. She's just an air-head.'

'I know that,' I said. 'But what about the fact that she is the one who actually recruited Malcolm from Thailand? And I suppose you have conveniently forgotten that she is married on paper to the long-standing Israeli boss of this street-selling business in Kagoshima City. You know, the one you have been trying to nail for ten years, but have been unable to do so since he's married to a policeman's daughter. Seeing as she has obligingly signed your statement, you will also be aware that she has made countless millions of yen out of this business, not to mention the hundred thousand I handed over to her at the beginning of June. Don't you think all that means she deserves to be tied to a chair and interviewed along with me? Or does her empty-headedness as well as her parentage excuse her from having to be subjected to your flexible version of the Japanese legal system?'

Takada paused for some moments before answering feebly, 'She is also being interviewed from time to time.'

'Sure she is. The only difference in her case is that she can go home afterwards, when she has finished pouring her interviewers' green tea, that is!' I returned, unable to control my rage at such blatant double standards.

In my angry verbal outburst I had acknowledged, for the first time, my part in the handling of money, but it had been obvious from previous questions that they already knew about it. I was now aware that I had passed the point of no return but I was too tired to care. My position could hardly get worse, and I was no longer able to block all the evidence that led to Budo's door. Despite the inevitability of it all, I continued for the rest of the day to insist that Detective Inspector Takada and his colleagues would be better served looking in the direction of Malcolm's apartment if they wanted to find out the identity of a boss behind him. Of course, I knew that its history had already been traced back to the Guttersnipe and her husband. I also knew that the owner of the apartment was also the girlfriend of an older Japanese Kagoshima street-seller, so to point the police in that direction was not unreasonable, although, it was not at all what Takada wanted to hear.

On the way back to my cell, Takada recommended that I have a good think about my situation, because the way things were going, he was not very optimistic about my future. On parting, he and Yamazaki kindly promised to raise a few glasses for me that night. I was left with the dilemma of betraying a trusted and loyal friend, or opting for a probable gaol sentence – hardly the ideal subject for contemplation on the night of your thirtieth birthday, especially without a crate of beer at hand.

1st July

The new month started much the same as the old one, only this morning Takada took some time in getting his papers together before joining us in the tiny investigation room. In that interval, I learnt that Malcolm, whom apparently everyone here knew as Joe, had indeed been deported, but had been allowed to go home without any fine or penalty for his offence. On top of this, he had left the country with over Y500,000 – that constituted everything he had saved from his two months on the street.

Takada spent the day drawing upon Malcolm's eventual co-operation and quoted various pieces of information with regard to the flow of merchandise, the mode of transport for work, and the financial arrangements. He claimed that they all led back to Budo; the van was taxed in his name, the accessories and boards had come from his house, and suspicious sums of money had been paid into his account. I made no comment at this stage, but for the first time, I was completely convinced that the police had all the proof they needed to close in on Budo, particularly as his own personal car number plate had been recorded in Kagoshima at the most critical times.

I had confirmed in a previous statement – based on my general knowledge of the street-selling system – that the worker was likely to have received a cut of thirty-five per cent from the gross, with any expenses such as parking and accommodation being his responsibility. The overriding feeling on the third floor of the police station was that Malcolm had been exploited and had unwittingly become caught up in something he knew nothing about. I, on the other hand, did not entirely share their sympathy, and felt compelled to point out that travellers like Malcolm are only too pleased to work for a couple of months in a job such as this without the strings or responsibilities of conventional working contracts attached. They just want to make enough money to live off for the rest of the year in a cheaper part of Asia. Naturally the bosses make a killing, but it's a two-way thing, (and it's up to the police to get off their backsides to do something about it, I added in English to myself, sanctimoniously). My feelings towards this business had always been conflicting to the point of hypocrisy.

Whilst on the subject, I mentioned that Malcolm's sister had apparently made a fortune in six months of working for the Guttersnipe, and her husband's *basta* business in Kagoshima. Being a foreign female seller in a homogeneous society in which western pornographic videos abounded, but which only had a handful of Filipino prostitutes, can be quite an attraction, not to mention a selling point. The drunk Japanese male's weakness for such a seller soon manifests itself in a curious glance at her wares and then his inevitable, 'How much?' represents double entendre in its crudest sense.

At this point, Yamazaki san piped up, 'Funny you should say that, because I once shelled out Y3,000 in much the same circumstances to a foreign seller down in Miyakonojo.'

Detective Inspector Takada shot him such a look that, by rights, he should have dropped dead on the spot. A double blow for the senior policeman, having just learnt that Malcolm was also not quite as innocent as he had pretended to be.

None of this however, altered my situation, as Takada san later pointed out when we were left alone. For perhaps the first time, he came across as more human than policeman when he assured me that he felt a greater affinity to me than to Malcolm – probably, he added, because I spoke his language. If I helped him, he said, he would do his best to help me. He said that as a detective he realised that it was often difficult for suspects to tell the whole truth due to loyalty or whatever, but that in my case, I had reached the stage to be honest for the sake of my future. Again, he urged me to think long and hard that night; to make sure I did the sensible thing.

Back in my cell that night, I was tired of the whole affair, but in a way I was relieved, because I had decided to admit my part in the street business. The mountain of evidence against Budo was already so overwhelming that I felt nothing I could say could make the consequences any worse for him. Besides, it was now time for me to think of myself.

3rd July

The day before, I had filled in the gaps that – as Yamazaki san euphemistically put it – I had previously not remembered correctly. I certainly felt much better for it, and the junior detective seemed to be equally relieved, while Takada had attacked his typewriter with renewed vigour.

However, the tendency to negatively oversimplify my statement had continued: 'I agreed to help out behind the scenes in as far as it was convenient for me,' became, 'I agreed to be the Kagoshima street-shop manager in place of Mishak.' Budo's 'spontaneous decision to open up his shop while we were travelling through Kokubu City one night in early March,' was turned into, 'And there the Kagoshima street business started.' I was glad that Mr Ishikubo read back the translations to me at the end of each day to give me a chance to limit the damage. Takada was annoyed by my concern with the 'slight differences in nuance', as he chose to term them, and told me that they were insignificant in relation to the overall case.

That Thursday morning, as Hamadome san put my cuffs on and led me on the rope to the transfer point, he told me that today I was going for a little drive. He was right, for Takada and a dozen other detectives were waiting to escort me to Kokubu City, as apparently they wanted me to show them the exact route that had been taken and precisely where the accessory shop had been set up. Eight of them packed around one manacled Englishman in a police van, with two cars following, seemed somewhat excessive by any standards. It again begged the question of exactly how much real crime there was in Kagoshima.

The National Route 10 coastal road took on a whole new aura of beauty and freedom. Mt Sakurajima, as usual, stood magnificently in the background, the thin plume of light grey smoke above it belying its awesome latent volcanic power. The ocean, a sparkling blue under the radiant sunshine, appeared to be calling me to swim, though it was still far too early by Japanese rules. Nobody spoke in the van. Maybe we were all momentarily freeing ourselves from our current realities.

We arrived in Kokubu City an hour and a half later. I indicated the night-life building as well as the location of the *basta* just inside, opposite the sushi shop. The detectives, with their extremely serious faces, then made an elaborate performance of energetically marking the area with chalk and meticulously measuring its precise dimensions after consulting me as to whether it was a millimetre this way or that. They then took a video film and numerous photographs from various angles of me standing in the position of the stall and car parking spaces, my handcuffs disguised by a large black mitten, and a small policeman holding my rope whilst hiding behind me to avoid the lenses.

In the midst of such frenetic police activity I wondered, not for the first time, whether perhaps I had inadvertently murdered a couple of people along the way. In the van on the way back, I racked my brains to think when it could possibly have been.

4th July

With the arrival of my improved memory, emerged a less intimidating Detective Inspector Takada. Before, the prospect of a prison sentence or at best, immediate deportation with a heavy fine had been intimated. Now, there was talk of an early release and even a post-custodial drink, but naturally, he could not guarantee anything. He would, however, recommend to the chief prosecutor that I be treated lightly in view of what he called my 'fine record' in Japan before the more recent misdemeanour.

I recalled my previous trip to the prosecutor's office and expressed my concern to the two detectives.

'I wish I hadn't tried to be clever with the little chap on my last visit. It's just that he was so rude.'

'Yes, we heard about that,' said Takada with a smile.

'Don't worry about it,' said Yamazaki soothingly. 'You just dared to put into words what everyone who meets him thinks. It's the poor lad on the word processor that I feel most sorry for. He has to suffer the length of his tongue every other minute, six days a week.'

'That's the problem with very small men – I call them Small Boys, or S.B. for short – they've always got a chip on their shoulder,' remarked Takada.

'As long as you remember to show "Hansei" (deep remorse) for your actions, that is the most important thing in Japan,' advised Yamazaki.

This was yet another new item of Japanese vocabulary for me to add to my collection. It apparently carried far more weight than the common word for regret which I knew as 'koukai'. I resolved to store it away for later use.

*

That morning I was taken by van once again to the prosecutor's office. My first block of ten days was almost up and I was hoping that I would soon be able to put the experience behind me. The young prison guard, Hamadome san, had given me grounds for optimism earlier when he did up my handcuffs, saying that he thought I was about to be released.

Time in the barred waiting room seemed interminable, with all the Japanese prisoners being called before I was, just like on the previous occasion. The individual with the goat-beard was the last one left in with me. I almost did not recognise him, because today he was clean-shaven. Despite his never having wanted to speak to me, I could not help commenting upon his new image.

'Japan is all about impressions and appearances,' he told me. 'The bottom line is that I am a member of the *yakuza*. This immediately goes against me with the authorities. Anything I can do to soften this hard impression, like shave off my beard or go through the motions of *hansei* in front of the judge, I will. At the end of the day, we all just want to get out of here as fast as possible.'

My sentiments precisely, I thought, but I did not really fancy his chances, since the Japanese police were apparently starting to crack down hard on drug dealers.

S.B. seemed to be in a much better mood today. He was courteous to me, and he only scolded his assistant on the word processor twice. He went through my typed statements efficiently, giving a summary as before, and asking me pre-prepared questions where necessary. One of these focused on my motive for coming to Japan that February. I said truthfully that I wanted to attend a football team-mate's wedding party, to study karate, to re-enter the English-teaching world (I had attended an interview in early June), and to add to my Japanese experiences with a view to writing a book. He then asked me directly if Budo had asked me to be boss of the Kagoshima street-business. I replied that we had discussed it and that I had said I would help behind the scenes only when it suited me, which is exactly what I had told Detectives Takada and Yamazaki.

When the chief prosecutor had finished asking questions about the Guttersnipe's contractual marriage – about which I knew nothing – and had resolved to interview her another day, he asked me politely if I would care to make any comments. Although I was aggrieved at the blatant injustices of the case and, for that matter, the fact that I was here at all, I had accepted my situation and had realised that my prime objective was to get out into the fresh air again as soon as possible. With this in mind, I merely apologised humbly for having wasted his valuable time on the previous occasion, throwing in a *hansei* for good measure. He in turn, said very graciously that it was all part of his job, and bowed politely to signal my dismissal. I tried to do likewise but had overlooked the fact that I was tied to my chair.

★

The news came through to my cell later that I had been condemned to another ten days. I stared out at the *tako-yaki* shop dejectedly.

7th July

It had been a long weekend, punctuated only by meal times and Tiger Woods. There had been no *o-shirabe* because Detectives Takada and Yamazaki had taken the weekend off. Time had hung very heavily indeed and I was actually quite pleased to see them when they showed up to collect me at quarter past nine that Monday morning. They both apologised for not coming in to relieve my boredom. I tried to imagine a police officer in Britain excusing himself to his prisoner for taking time off, and had to laugh at the absurdity of such a thought.

When seated comfortably in the interview room, Takada told me that had I recalled events more clearly earlier, I would probably have avoided this second ten day sentence. Objectively speaking, it seemed a fair comment. He then went on to quiz me in intimate detail about the financial elements of the case. I was unable to recall the exact days that I had collected money from Malcolm's apartment, but told them that I had done it several times a week. I did know, however, that I had looked after the money until the end of each of the two month periods, when I had physically handed it over to Budo, first in Kumamoto and the second time in Kagoshima. From this I had received two payments; one amounting to just under Y120,000, and the second, just under Y200,000, making a combined total of about £1,600, which was only just over half of what Malcolm had walked out of Japan with – hardly the kind of salary a boss would expect.

'How did you feel about receiving such payments?' asked Takada.

'I felt, and still feel perfectly at ease with my conscience.' I responded defensively. 'I often found it a real chore having to run around after Malcolm, particularly in the first week when, naturally, he couldn't do a thing by himself. Collecting and looking after the money on behalf of Budo was also a nuisance, so of course I felt entitled to remuneration – any normal human-being would.'

'Legally speaking, I mean,' persisted Takada.

'The money was not stolen, Mr Takada. It was earned honestly on the street from Japanese citizens who choose to buy these accessories of their own free will from such sellers every day of the week throughout Japan. I am sure you recall that even off-duty policemen are sometimes included in the clientele,' I glanced at Yamazaki, 'while the working officers, by and large, merely close their eyes to the trade.'

Detective Inspector Takada listened impassively but made no effort to commit any of these observations to the written word. He did, on the other hand, get busy with the typewriter when I confirmed that Budo was supposed to be passing on Y400,000 to Mishak for the monthly rental of the city, out of which apparently the Guttersnipe was to receive Y150,000 in accordance with a clause in the marriage contract. I told them that my early June delivery to her of Y100,000 yen was at the request of Budo on behalf of Mishak, and was a one-off.

'Do you know if Budo actually sent Mishak this money both times?' enquired Yamazaki.

'I know that the first time there was not enough profit to send that amount due to all manner of expenses related to Malcolm's apartment. All I know is that Budo intended to make those payments. Whether he actually did or not, I have no idea,' I replied truthfully.

'Do you know who decided upon this monthly rental fee of Y400,000?' asked Takada, puzzled.

'I would imagine that Mishak did,' I hazarded. 'As you well know, it was common practice before for such self-appointed street bosses to hire workers to run shops in their cities. Now, many of these bosses have chosen to rent out their Japanese cities from the comfort of Israel. Of course, their profits are greatly reduced, but they have already made a nice little nest egg and are content to live off of this hassle-free regular income.'

I resisted the temptation to indicate Nagasaki's Sasebo City as another typical example. There, I knew for a fact that Mike was grudgingly transferring almost $2,000 a month to a bank in Israel for the privilege of setting out his *basta* in the city. Our last conversation had revealed that he had nevertheless saved almost £100,000 in two and a half years and was now considering retirement at the age of thirty.

The investigation centred on the money side of things all day, and I was again returned to my cell for supper feeling quite drained. The radio was turned on at around six o'clock playing its usual selection of tuneless songs. Just as the inmates' Kagoshima daily newspaper was always subjected to rigorous censorship by the prison authorities, the radio news was always switched off by the guards. This evening, however, the local radio newscaster boomed out the arrest of Kumamoto, Nagamine-machi's Isaac Goldstein – Budo's real name – in connection with a foreign street-selling ring, before two frantic guards raced to turn it off. I was not the only one to hear the news item, so it appeared that Budo was not alone in heading for the high-jump.

8th July

Early that morning, shortly before ten to seven, eight of us were led upstairs, past the back of the second floor cells, on the way to our daily exercise plot. Curled up in the embryo position on the floor of room Number Nine, was the unmistakable shaven-headed figure of Budo.

'Shalom, Isaac!' I cried in one of my four words of Hebrew.

My Jewish friend instantly sprang up like a cat and asked urgently, 'Luke! Are you all right?'

I barely had time to assure him that I was, before the guard shoved me in the back and shouted that English was forbidden in this prison.

Outside on the roof, the band of smokers was animatedly discussing the new *gai-jin* arrival as well as the previous evening's radio broadcast. I was walking back and forth, away from their smoke, in my usual spot up the far end, thinking how good it had been to see a friendly face for the first time in fourteen days. The previous Friday, a police chief had entered the investigation room to hand me a slip of paper with seven names on it. Apparently, my friends from the football team were worried and had been making enquiries after me. It was surprising how those seven names, though written by a Japanese hand, almost made me choke with emotion when I read them.

As Yamazaki san sensitively put it, 'Your friends have not discarded you. At least you know you're not alone.'

At the same time, I had been informed that the British Embassy had phoned enquiring after my health to which the police had apparently replied simply that I was 'Genki' (well). It later emerged that a consular official by the name of Ms Osama had asked again if I would like to be visited after my stay in custody had been extended. The Kagoshima police representative had apparently told her that I had refused this offer.

On the way back in, Budo was waiting at the back of his cell like a caged animal.

'Have you made a confession?' he asked urgently.

'They know almost everything,' I answered quickly, as I passed on down the locker-room corridor, thinking how stupid it was of the police to lock us up in the same place.

I later found out that my two interviewing detectives shared my opinion. They spent the day quizzing me on the various *basta* boards and merchandise that were now all lined up in the spacious office next door. It seemed they had transported Budo's stall down from Kumamoto as well.

I smiled, as I could imagine the scene at the moment they had laid a finger on that, knowing how the Jew cherished the stuff of his trade as if it were his very own daughter. The burly, sour-faced detective, whom I had not talked to for some time, implied that Budo had indeed not come quietly by the words, 'Goldstein wa ki ga mijikai ne,' ('He's got a short temper').

He then went on to cast a couple more aspersions; the first being that Budo was a 'stingy bastard' and the second that Malcolm was a 'stiff, hopeless seller'. I laughed, just about managing to resist making a generalised racist comment about the first and agreeing with the second.

During the course of the afternoon I was told that all being well, I might be released that Friday, and that I would probably be allowed to stay in Japan until my visa naturally expired towards the end of August. This was good news, and my mind automatically raced to my mental note of my football team's fixture list... A league game on Sunday – perfect!

10th July

The previous afternoon I had been surprised to catch a glimpse of Rumi, Robert's wife, in the next-door police departmental office. Detective Yamazaki told me that she would be standing surety for my release and had come to fill in the necessary papers. It came as a huge relief to see that the ball was actually rolling in the direction of my freedom, but my cynical side refused to let me get too excited while I was still this side of the prison fence.

Takada continued to question me about Budo's business in Kumamoto. He was interested to know about his merchandise. I told him that it was largely purchased from Korea and Thailand but that since I had never accompanied him on his buying missions, I knew little more than that. Another, more serious looking detective named Kinoshita entered the interview room at this stage, brandishing Budo's personal pocket computer. I knew that this was where Budo stored a record of his daily takings for the last two years, and was able to confirm that this was the meaning of the list of figures that flashed up on the screen. Kinoshita tapped into the six week period covering early December to January, generally the most lucrative season in the Japanese street-selling calendar. It threw up a total exceeding Y3,000,000, which invited all four of us to conclude that we were in the wrong job.

'Of course he does pay tax on it, you know, which really is somewhat inconsistent with the view that the business is illegal,' I remarked, more as a point of fact than an attempt to be clever.

The comment drew no response, and Takada passed smoothly on to his next query.

'Is your friend involved in any other kind of business?'

'Such as?' I replied, unable to grasp what he was getting at.

'I mean, does he sell anything else besides accessories?'

'Well, he has got this new line in laser pens; you know, those things that make people jump out of their skins at a distance of fifty feet.'

'Anything else?'

'If you are referring to drugs, Detective Inspector Takada, then I can assure you he does not deal in those. You know he was a policeman in the drug squad at Tel Aviv Airport, and his opinion of them, like his opinion of smoking, is exactly the same as mine.'

'What about telephone cards?' enquired Takada calmly.

This question took me rather by surprise, but I tried not to show it even though I suspected my face had reddened which it had an annoying tendency to do.

'He does not vend telephone cards,' I answered firmly.

'No, but he uses fake ones in Japanese phones, doesn't he? We know this because we came across a bundle when we searched his house. You know, the type that's held together with a rubber band.' Takada looked me straight in the eyes, the corner of his mouth rising slightly in an almost imperceptible smile, as it always did when he knew his question caused discomfort.

'It's common knowledge that you can purchase these from members of the underworld in any large city, but perhaps you had better ask him about that,' I suggested flatly.

'We intend to,' said Takada, getting up to go and retrieve his packet of cigarettes from his desk in the next room.

'Don't worry about the cards,' whispered Yamazaki. 'None were found on you, so there's no problem.'

Detective Kinoshita, who was still puzzling over Budo's pocket computer, asked me if I knew the coded names and addresses that flashed up. I pleaded ignorance, but actually I recognised most of them as abbreviated forms of the names of members of his network of *basta* friends, who were scattered all around Japan. Some of them I had even met, particularly one, who in April had come to Budo's house and had flaunted his fake passport at us while regaling me with stories of his criminal past. He had apparently spent several years in prison in the North of Kyushu, and after being deported, had arranged false identity papers in Thailand with which to re-enter Japan. This being successfully achieved, he continued to run a string of shops, despite being questioned again by Japanese police in connection with telephone cards. According to his tale, he was even asked face to face in the police station lift by his former investigator if he was indeed the same Israeli *gai-jin* he had sent down two years previously. Budo's friend had calmly denied this and managed to walk away a free man, thanking his lucky stars that, to the Japanese, all foreigners seem to look the same.

Later on that morning, a grey-haired detective, whom I knew only as Kachou, came in portentously holding an envelope that had been discovered in Budo's house. It was my Barclaycard Visa statement for April displaying a debt of £24. Little Kachou, however, suspected that it was a paper revealing some far greater corruption, and proceeded to bark out twenty related questions on the subject, going to the extreme of asking in which month of which year I had become a Barclaycard holder.

The afternoon saw an unexpected visit to the chief prosecutor's office. It was a fairly muddled affair in which S.B. asked questions that had already been answered in earlier statements. There was also confusion over the financial side of things, with apparently, a great deal being lost in the translation, although the poor girl who had replaced the first interpreter was undoubtedly doing her best. It ended with S.B. concluding that as I was only a helper in this business, my case would not go to a civil court but would be decided internally with the possibility of a small fine. To say that I was exceedingly pleased to hear this piece of news is an understatement.

I rode back in the prison minibus on a new high. One of the senior guards, called Nagata san, was also in talkative mood.

'So you were able to see the little chap again today, were you? I mean you could actually see him above the desk this time?'

I laughed, surprised at such a sniping comment but enjoying the sarcasm all the same.

'Yes, he seemed in a better mood again today,' I said.

'That's because you reminded him of his manners on your first encounter,' explained Nagata.

'Oh, you know about that?' I asked, genuinely surprised.

'Everybody does. It's not often the bad-tempered little turd gets spoken to like that. Anyway, I hear you'll be out soon.'

'Yes, if I can pay my fine. I might be coming to you for a loan, though,' I joked.

'That's all right. I think I can manage the small amount your fine is likely to be,' he replied seriously.

'How much is small?' I asked.

'Usually between Y100,000 and Y300,000,' he replied. 'You can soon get that back with a bit of private teaching. Talking of which, I've got an eighteen-year-old daughter who wants to go on to study English at college. She's got enormous breasts, you know,' he boasted gesticulating wildly. 'How about giving her a private lesson or two?'

I was not sure whether I was the only one registering a large helping of double entendre, as most of the other guards were keeping a straight face, so I just said, 'I am sure we can sort something out.'

By now we had arrived back at Chuo Police Station. As Nagata san led me out on my rope, he continued, 'Be sure to give me a call as soon as you are released and we'll go out on the town. I'll give you my number when you come for your next hearing.'

With that, I was led back to the detention area by two of his junior guards, feeling more than ready to mark my return to society with a drink or two.

11th July

Earlier that week, for some reason, I had been moved up to Budo's room and he had been moved down to mine. I could not quite see the logic behind the exchange because it only meant that he passed my room when going out for his morning exercise instead of me passing his, so naturally we still managed a fleeting, garbled conversation.

That particular morning in the yard, I was feeling uncharacteristically positive, but did not tell anybody else the reason for this. I chatted for the first time with the old man, who had always kept himself to himself. The only thing I knew about him was that he was on a course of medication that the guards brought him religiously every evening. All the younger inmates were constantly speculating as to what sort of heinous crime he had committed, and some had even had the cheek to ask him directly, though he never answered. It turned out that he was from the city of Kanoya, a place where I had spent many happy evenings during my first year in Japan as an English teacher. He confessed that he was dreading going back there as, being a country town, rumours there had spread like wildfire and he was too ashamed to show his face again. I knew exactly what he meant.

Takada came to fetch me at about ten in the morning but did not have anything in particular to ask me, so we spent an hour or so talking about life in general. He said that he realised how monotonous time must be in the prison cell, so he thought that bringing me over for a little chat might help to kill a bit of time. He predicted that my release would probably not take place today and that the fact that there was no word from S.B.'s office made it increasingly likely that it would be delayed until Monday. He later reported that Budo was not co-operating, and suggested that when I next managed to sneak a few words with him, I might like to urge him to admit his involvement so the case could be speedily tied up. One of the other detectives joked that they would pay me Y10,000 an hour to translate for him, because apparently even the police translator was having trouble understanding his mixture of English and Japanese. I could not help laughing, as Budo was the only person in my circle of friends who had the potential to order lunch in a Japanese restaurant and end up being served a tractor.

Yamazaki also popped in for a short time. We discussed the recent typhoons, one of which had caused a landslide in neighbouring Izumi City, killing twenty people. I knew full well that the local police were often very busy dealing with such natural disasters, because Kagoshima was also a frequent victim of earthquakes, not to mention its susceptibility to the moods of its resident active volcano, Sakurajima. In addition to these problems, apparently, the city's port police constantly had their work cut out tackling the *yakuza*'s frequent operations to smuggle Chinese immigrants in by boat. On a lighter, more vulgar note, Yamazaki posed a question that he had apparently been dying to ask a foreigner since he was a little boy; which was whether people from abroad could simultaneously urinate and take a crap, because seemingly, unlike most races, Japanese people could.

I was returned to my cell at quarter past eleven, just in time for The Peasant to indulge in his favourite trick of taking everybody's weekend snack order except mine. I buried myself in my book until I was collected once again by Detective Inspector Takada, who took me back to his office for cakes and two cups of coffee. He revealed that my fine would be Y200,000 and that if I authorised it, he would pass Rumi my cash-card so that she could arrange the money for Monday. This I did, and spent the next half an hour discussing my post-penal plans with a man who had miraculously been transformed from Japanese police tyrant into thoroughly decent human being. Amazing the difference three weeks can make, I thought to myself.

14th July

The weekend had dragged by, but I did succeed in rationing the chapters of the Michael Crichton book to last until Sunday afternoon. The only two notable moments had come when a fellow shaver had asked me to comment on speculation among the inmates that I was a drug baron, and when Budo had stolen into the bath-house to ask me exactly how much the police knew. To the first question, I answered that with remarks like that there was more chance of me being convicted of murder and to the second, I hardly had time to say anything before he was dragged out by the scruff of his neck in the midst of a lot of angry shouting. The obvious low point had been missing out on Sunday's league game for my team, The Habu.

I got up rather excitedly that Monday morning. As usual, there were a handful of plain-clothed police officers supervising the ritual of putting the futons away and cleaning the rooms. There was a little individual with a handlebar moustache and a dark complexion grinning away at me from behind the meshed bars at the back of my cell.

'Where abouts are you from in America?' he asked in a cheerful voice.

'I'm from London, England,' I replied trying to keep matters simple.

'Really? I went to London with my wife on our honeymoon, you know – we only stopped in Heathrow Airport actually, in transit. Mind you, I was ever so pleased because I managed to have a photograph taken standing next to one of your British bobbies. They are so tall and wear such smart uniforms. It was the highlight of my holiday.'

This last statement either told me a lot about his dedication to his job or even more about his wife. I thanked him for the compliment and chatted a little while longer about travelling abroad before he trotted off to begin his work.

The hours up to lunchtime seemed interminable, and with nothing to read, I could only pace my cell. It came as a relief when at about one o'clock one of the younger guards, who wore glasses, led me out to my locker area and returned all my personal possessions. I signed for them after checking that the remaining cash was correct after the automatic subtraction of the payment for my bread, soap and toothbrush. I was also ecstatic to see my ring which I immediately put on, but I was advised to leave the belt in my bag until I was outside the prison. Before being led out to the van, I managed to have a shouted last few words with Budo from my cell, during which I suggested that there was little point his remaining silent if he wanted to get out, since the police knew everything already. He agreed, and said that he would talk once I had been released. We wished each other good luck, and I was off on my way to the prosecutor's office for what I hoped would be the last time. I had thanked all of the prison guards, particularly Yoshinaga san and Hamadome san. I had even thanked The Peasant, who, true to form, had hissed a sarcastic, 'Sayonara!', doubtless one of the few words of standard language he had mastered.

In the barred waiting room, I exchanged a few words with a slightly older Japanese man, and when I asked him what he was in for, he simply replied, 'Kagoshima no keisatsu wa hima dakara.'

This was not the first time I had heard that the Kagoshima police have so much time on their hands that they pull people in for even the slightest infringement of the law.

My session in front of the chief prosecutor left me more baffled than anything else. Whereas from Takada san's news on Friday, I had assumed that everything was cut and dried, S.B. summed my case up and presented me with two courses of action: either to let an independent body at the small claims court deliberate over the appropriate size of my fine today; or to appeal against the judgement so far and refer it to a court panel some weeks later. Of course, I took the first option. S.B. then informed me that this would take some time, and that I would have to wait patiently for the result. I told him that this was no problem, apologised again for wasting his time and was led back down to the waiting room.

During the next two hours, I had a good look at all the pornographic magazines and paced the three-metre room at least a hundred times before being led by the guards up to a different room full of bureaucrats at about five o'clock. There I was informed through the interpreter that the decision had just come through that I was liable to a fine of Y200,000. I concluded that the earlier act in the prosecutor's office had merely been a case of observing the set formalities.

We then proceeded out across the courtyard and into another building, where I could see Rumi and Robert making a transaction over the counter. I was pleased at last to be free of my handcuffs, which I had been relieved of earlier. This reduced my humiliation only slightly as I thanked the interpreter and made my way over to Robert.

'How did you get on in yesterday's game?' I enquired eagerly.

'Oh, we won 5-4,' replied Robert jubilantly.

'Thank the Lord for that!' I said with a huge sigh of relief.

*

A night of *yaki-niku* (grilled beef) and beer at Robert's house with Rumi and a couple of the lads from the football team was just what the doctor ordered. It was excellent to be back in the outside world. The experience of the previous three weeks immediately felt like a detached part of some distant reality. It was great to be able to speak normal English again, and a real revelation to hear about the efforts my friends had gone to in order to try and break down the impenetrable Kagoshima police investigation process.

The utter inflexibility and pettiness of the system were underlined by the police chief's uncompromising attitude towards my being allowed some reading matter. Apparently, he had informed Robert that if I wanted a Bible, he would have to pay for it, which Robert replied that he would do. On hearing that, the police chief decided that it would have to be a Japanese Bible, so that the prison wardens could check that there was nothing relevant to my case written inside – a quick conversion from Buddhist to Christian seemed more likely than that a Japanese guard would wade through all one thousand two hundred and ninety one pages!

I was also interested to learn that a meeting had been held between the veteran members of The Habu and the bosses of Chuo Police Station. One of the main subjects raised was why the day after my arrest my name had been splashed all over the newspaper, the article depicting me as the boss of the Kagoshima Street-selling racket before the police had bothered even to find out whether it was true or not.

Robert had apparently asked, 'What happens if you find out he is innocent of your charges?'

Then had come the diabolically lame response:

'It's the newspaper's fault. We cannot control what they print.'

Boisterous laughter from the lads signified another own-goal by the police. How many other sources for such an article were there, for goodness sake?

★

The next morning, with a for once welcome hangover, I went along to the local park on the back of Robert's motorbike for a kickaround. The following Sunday would see the Kagoshima section of the Toyota Cup soccer tournament, and after three weeks of walking in stretches of no more than three metres, I had a lot of fitness to win back, and some re-acclimatising to do; the rainy season had officially finished so the days had reverted to bright sunshine with nearly eighty per cent humidity. I had to take things easy because in that short space of time, I had lost five kilogrammes.

The air was clean and fresh, the grass as luscious as always on the plateau below the park's artificial rocket and above Hirakawa Zoo. The call of the wild; the fragrance of a colourful array of roses, the effortless gliding of an overhead bird of prey, all the natural elements we smugly take for granted, today assumed for me a special magic power. Even the football received my grateful acknowledgement, as it helped speed my passage back to normality. However, it was impossible to put my recent experience totally behind me, as while I was in the shower back at Robert's, Sergeant Nagata phoned Robert's house asking to speak to me about that drink, and his daughter's English lessons, no doubt.

When I got back to my apartment that evening, I found an envelope full of beer coupons from Detective Yamazaki, along with a kind note. Half an hour later, there came a tap on the window, and I nearly jumped out of my skin when I saw Detective Inspector Takada's face, with Yamazaki skipping around behind him.

'How about that drink I promised you?' suggested the older man.

'Why not?' I replied, not feeling any particular malice towards him.

At that precise moment, my landlord passed and visibly cringed when he saw the police on his property yet again.

Yamazaki san, who was still jigging around in some state of excitement, was quick to reassure him that all was well: 'Daijoobu desu. Mo tomodachi ni natte kita.' ('It's all right, we're friends now'). The two detectives explained to me where we were to drink, drew me a rough map and arranged to meet me there at seven o'clock.

I arrived at Yachan Izakaya just before seven. To my pleasant surprise, Mr Ishikubo, the translator who had checked over all the nuance differences of my Japanese statements each day, was there with the detectives. We took up our place on the *tatami* side of the establishment, where we toasted life itself and tucked into platefuls of succulent *kushi-yaki* (skewered meat). Predictably, the conversation was somewhat strained until the beer started to flow, and then Takada inevitably made reference to my three week stint behind bars with the dismissive summary, 'Taishita koto nakatta,' ('It was no big deal').

I stuck my pint jockey glass into my mouth and took a long hard swig so that I would be able to suppress my urge to question why, in that case, the Kagoshima police had made such a big deal out of it. He went on to ask me what my biggest criticism of the whole affair was, to which I replied:

'Letting the newspapers print slanderous articles about my being the boss, while your office hypocritically covered up the far greater and long-standing involvement of a fellow police officer's daughter.'

'Yeah, yeah, besides that?'

I looked at him with raised eyebrows, unsure how to react to his flagrant trivialisation of such a crucial point.

He continued indifferently, 'I was convinced your major complaint would be the lack of English books. A valid grievance, I might add. We must do something about that in time for the next foreigner.'

Yamazaki and Ishikubo sat in silence. I emptied the meat plate along with my glass and banged it down to signal I was ready for another.

Total alcoholic intoxication at the detective inspector's expense seemed to be the only path to self-appeasement.

There were a couple more rungs on the drinking ladder at nearby *izakayas*. In the first, we listened to some fascinating stories from Mr Ishikubo's days in Africa, and in the second, the others having made their excuses, I enjoyed a quiet heart-to-heart with Mr Yamazaki, who apparently longed to return to the more intimate life of country policing. We were then collected by his wife, who rose from her bed at his call to drive the thirty minutes from Kajiki City, and I was dropped off at my apartment in the early hours of the morning. On the door was a note from PC Suzuki saying that he had popped around for a drink, and asking me to call him.

Epilogue

Budo was released on Monday, 28th July. His spell in custody and his fine were identical to mine. The police returned all of his *basta* equipment with his merchandise and he went straight back to the streets of Kumamoto to continue where he had left off. His friend Minami, the big *yakuza* boss from the *Yamaguchi-gumi* group rushed up to hug him after his recent ordeal, while the rest of the *sakariba*'s underworld characters bowed deeply with new-found respect. Budo's regular customers flocked to his stall, and in the first five days of re-opening, he took Y500,000.

During that same period at the end of July, I was offered a teaching position at a private school in Kagoshima Prefecture. I was about to sign the contract on 30th July, when a large article appeared that very same day in the Minami-Nihon Newspaper to scupper the whole arrangement. It focused on my descent from the heights of a successful teaching career on the Osumi peninsular in 1989, to the depths of so-called villainy on the Satsuma peninsular in 1997. It also gave passing mention to Budo but there was nothing about the police officer's daughter.

Over the next couple of weeks, I received a number of invitations to go drinking with certain men of the law, including Detective Kinoshita who along with Detective Yamazaki, took me to a beer garden and then on to four more rungs of the *hashigo* thereafter. Apparently, they were both worried that I would leave Japan with a bad impression and, like Detective Inspector Takada, were eager to brighten the memory – or deaden it, at least. I did not bother telling them about the rumour that an influential *yakuza* with strong connections in the police had ordered that the foreign *basta* competition in Kagoshima be eradicated so that the Japanese sellers' profits would increase. A trip down the arcade later revealed them doing a roaring trade, as evidently they had been doing, unhampered, since the day after Malcolm's arrest. My two drinking companions made a joke that I might like to set out my stall – in an attempt to cover their obvious embarrassment.